Sexual Violence and American Manhood

Sexual Violence and American Manhood

T. Walter Herbert

Harvard University Press
Cambridge, Massachusetts,
and London, England

2002

Library of Congress Cataloging-in-Publication Data

Herbert, T. Walter (Thomas Walter), 1938–
Sexual violence and American manhood / T. Walter Herbert.
p. cm.
Includes bibliographical references and index.
ISBN 0-674-00917-7 (alk. paper)
1. Women—Violence against—United States.   2. Violence in men—United States.
3. Masculinity—United States.   4. Sex role—United States.
5. Men—United States—Psychology.   I. Title.

HV6250.4.W65 .H463 2002
305.3—dc21   2002068833

For my daughter, Crate

Contents

Sexual Violence and
American Manhood

Prologue

My first encounter with violent pornography took place in the Eastern Seaboard Railway Station at Waldo, Florida, about twenty miles from Gainesville, where we lived. My family had moved to Florida when I entered the third grade, just after World War II, so I was well acquainted with other worlds. My mother had grown up in Pennsylvania, spending the school months in Philadelphia and summers on her grandparents' farm near Gettysburg. My father's family were South Carolinians. At that time the North and the South were more remote from each other than they are today, as indeed were other regions of the United States. Television, superhighways, and the jet airplane were still unknown; long-distance telephoning was expensive and the connections were bad.

When my father joined the navy in 1943, my mother took a job teaching sociology at Wilson College in Chambersburg, Pennsylvania. I spent a lot of time on trains during those years. The stationmaster at Waldo, reeling off the names of cities along the rail-line north, seemed like a magician summoning familiar spirits. The train was called the Silver Meteor, and on the rear door of the last car was painted a star trailing sparks in a black void. I remember fixing my eyes on this little icon when the train pulled away, and watching until it vanished from sight. Then I came back to my reality of sandy soil and clattering palm fronds. I never missed a chance to go over to Waldo.

I was twelve years old in 1951, when we went to meet guests arriving from the North. It was hot and the train was late, so we took refuge in a little diner attached to the waiting room, where we had Cokes. As my parents fell into grown-up conversation, I wandered over to a rotating bookstand and noticed a paperback whose cover featured a man in a double-breasted belted raincoat, with his hat pulled down over his eyes. I was flipping through the book when my eyes fell on the following passage:

> She staggered back a step and I yanked with the hand that held her dress and it came off in one piece with a quick loud tear, leaving her gasping and hurt . . . I slid my belt off and let it dangle from my hand. I watched her face. I saw the gamut of emotions flash by in quick succession, leaving a startled expression of pure animal terror . . . A naked woman and a leather belt. I looked at her, so bare and so pretty . . . legs spread apart to hold a precarious balance, a flat stomach hollowed under the fear that burned her body a faint pink, lovely smooth breasts, firm with terrible excitement, rising and falling with every gasping breath. (128–129)

I responded to this with a compound of sexual arousal and dread. I had momentarily lost contact with my surroundings, and was relieved to see that my parents were still chatting as before. The passage had taken me by surprise. The title and author (*One Lonely Night*, by Mickey Spillane) then meant nothing to me; if I had immediately returned the book to the rack, I later thought, I might have escaped the sickness. But I hadn't done that; I had reread the excerpt I've quoted, and soon had looked for similar passages.

I begin with an exercise in the archaeology of memory because the chapters to follow treat the sexual experience of men as a cultural legacy, which we inherit from the past. What befell me at the midpoint of the twentieth century—in a train station now long defunct—was no less personal for being historical, no less historical for being personal.

In the feminist consciousness-raising of the sixties women sought freedom from ingrained habits of subservience that they had come to feel were natural and right. Women freed themselves from themselves: they set their personal stories in an historical context and learned to understand spontaneous impulses as the outcome of social arrangements. "The women's movement has drawn inescapable and illuminating connections," wrote Adrienne Rich in 1971, "between our sexual lives and our political institutions" (167).

Growing boys likewise internalize models of manhood that shape the landscape on which we take our bearings day by day.

Yet the traditions that make us men enter the textures of individual experience by stealth, and understanding them requires uncovering the reality behind a deceptive surface drama. We are only beginning to understand the political structures and cultural traditions hidden within masculine experience and to challenge their logic.

I have described the moment in the Waldo train station as I remember it, and the little narrative suggests several of the inadequate explanations I have accepted, at one time and another, for the allure that held me. Is pornography magic, with an inherent hypnotic power? It certainly felt that way at the time: one moment I was casually looking through the paperbacks; the next moment I was swept into lurid imaginings. For a while it seemed plausible that pornography victimizes its readers by pouring a contaminant into their otherwise robust minds, and causes actual sexual violence against women in much the same way. I later adopted the idea that I had been trapped by the religious guilt pervading southern culture. My desire for a silver meteor to carry me north then seemed like a yearning for sexual self-affirmation, and my response to pornography a healthy impulse twisted by neurotic self-loathing. I had merely entertained a fantasy, after all, and had injured no one. But fantasies of sexual coercion still seemed morally troublesome, degrading to the fancied victim and also to me.

The most deceptive feature of that moment was its tense solitude, as though the blending of cruelty and desire were an intimate matter, whether of evil magic, personal sinfulness, or primal instinct. The moment was secretive, as such moments generally are, but not private. My fascination with Spillane was shared by millions of readers, and his writing strengthened a genre of explicit sexual violence in American popular culture that now spreads across the nation in countless books, magazines, videos, and films. *One Lonely Night* was republished in the 1990s, with other "Spillane Classics," in a fortieth anniversary edition.

Looking back, I can see that my experience of terrorized sexual arousal resembled that of the woman, even though the narrative placed me in the standpoint of the male aggressor. It invited me to share the snug bodily containment of the man in the belted trench coat, to become the poised ravisher holding the belt, who pauses to watch his victim tremble. Yet as the rush swept over me, I felt as though some assailant had stripped me bare and had left me gasping and abject. The scene depicted a panic that had dimly audible echoes in myself, even as I took the role of the male attacker.

Needless to say, this was much too complicated for a twelve-year-old to understand, though not too complicated for him to feel. How could I be the "woman" in this fantasy as strongly as the "man"? I could scarcely imagine such a thing until, many years later, I encountered Carol Clover's study of the modern horror film, which demonstrates that male viewers frequently project unacknowledged realities of male experience onto female characters who are targets of sexual attack.

Male supremacy is doubly active in violent porn. It is enacted by the abuse of the female figure by the male, but it also controls the way these figures are constructed. The canonical female victim—frightened and sexually aroused—is made to embody male experiences. She is a mirror that reflects a male predicament back into male eyes as though that predicament belongs to a woman rather than a man. The pornographic script empties women of their womanly qualities and replaces them with male qualities that men do not recognize as their own.

The sexual violence within sexist manhood works through an imaginative life that violates women first by excluding them from the work of defining womanhood and then by portraying them as embodiments of what men disavow. The self we men acknowledge is the central figure in a story we tell ourselves about ourselves, which is tailored to fit the standards by which our society permits us to claim masculine self-respect. The distresses of living enter the conventional story as tests of manhood, and the story includes standardized scenes depicting the joy of victory and the agony of defeat. But when defeat is built into the test itself, and necessarily befalls both winners and losers, then the specter of chronic failure pursues all the contestants. The resultant anxieties cannot be acknowledged directly, since doing so would prove that the test is bogus; but those anxieties must nonetheless be allayed. Fantasied scenarios of conquest in sexual encounters—the whole gamut from implicit coercion to outright assault—are narrative devices, if you are a man, that provide covert reassurance that your story remains the story of a man, when you are haunted by the suspicion that it is becoming the story of a woman.

To please such men—even to survive in the society we create—women become female impersonators. It's the same with "niggers," as Ralph Ellison observes in *Invisible Man*. White people invented "niggers" for reasons of their own; African Americans have to fake it.

Women can achieve only a fleeting approximation of the pornographic feminine, even in its milder forms. Rita Hayworth, whose portrayal of Gilda made her the "love goddess" of the 1940s, explained her many divorces and failed affairs by saying "men go to bed with Gilda, but wake up with me" (Leaming 122). The suicide of Marilyn Monroe likewise testifies to the melancholy of women trapped—and what American woman is not trapped?—in the psychic economy of the sex symbol. This feminine essence is a male elixir, distilled from male fluids and given back to the man as though it were the gift of another, or a prize he has won. Only when such an enchantment fades away can a relationship develop between a woman and a man that engages their real lives; yet the death of the enchantment often terminates the relationship.

How do men get locked—with all our social power—into a style of manhood that visits abuse on women, even as it alienates us from ourselves? How does the enchantment bind us, so that men live their inner lives through the bodies and emotions of women? The story of Adam and Eve captures the patriarchal situation with a minimum of fuss: the woman's body is made from a man. In American society a strong tradition holds that a woman is a person in her own right, even though men are startled when women act as though this is really true.

My experience of sex, like that of most American boys, was given form by sexism; yet I do not look back across a half-century at my youthful desire without nostalgia, and without recognizing that I was carried by that strong current into the relationships—with my wife and children—that mean the most in my adult life. With all its consternations, and the destruction too often implicated in its satisfaction, sexual vitality is a bedrock human strength.

My response to Mickey Spillane foretold that my sexual life would be inflected by a pornographic sensibility that had taken form in America roughly a century before, whose origin and development this book is devoted to analyzing. But the moment of pornographic enchantment itself, as Susan Griffin noted in *Pornography and Silence,* conceals the secret of its power (29–46). The processes of cross-gender identification were the farthest things from my mind in the Waldo train station.

This incident from my boyhood did not inaugurate a story of personal violence—sexual or otherwise—in my own life. I am a peaceable man, a college professor whose most recent involvement in physical conflict was a schoolyard fight (with a guy) when I was in the eighth grade. My wife of thirty-seven years has recently retired from the practice of family law, a career that I supported; my son and my daughter have made marriages in which both wives pursue careers and have kept their last names. Although I have been an ally to feminist initiatives at my college, I can't claim to be a paragon of pro-feminist virtue. I did not take a sufficient share in childcare and housekeeping in the early years, when my participation was most needed. My feminist commitments have been beneficial to me personally, on balance, partly through the financial strength that my wife's career brought the household, but most importantly because her professional achievements brought mutuality and equal standing to the center of our marriage.

What makes my personal story consequential is not that I've been the chief of sinners, with a story of redemption to offer. Nor have I suffered ostracism and professional losses because of taking part in the battle against family violence and sexual abuse. My story matters, if at all, because it is not exceptional.

The following chapters relate experiences drawn from my boyhood in the South and the twenty-five years I've lived in Texas. I've learned from conversations with therapists, judges, lawyers, officials in law enforcement and in college administration, domestic-abuse counselors, and convicted sex offenders. Most of these conversations I've pursued in the world that now surrounds me in the Southwest. This doubtless imparts a parochial viewpoint, and may tempt certain readers to conclude that the issues treated here pertain only to life in this region.

Still, I've come to believe that my southern boyhood has assisted my effort to understand sexual violence, because it has helped me see how social injustice (in particular race prejudice) enters the textures of intimate life. "They're like members of the family," white bigots used to say about African Americans, a remark that correctly—if unwittingly—likens the domination of blacks in the household to the intimate abuse of women. The Southwest is blighted by a tradition of violence that has been glamorized across the nation since the late nineteenth century, making Texas a screen on which the American dream of rugged self-reliant manhood has been projected. If there's a disadvantage in knowing this culture at first hand, there may also be special opportunities for insight into the style of masculinity that sponsors sexual violence.

At age twelve I was still a boy, looking ahead to manhood; and therein lies the keynote of the chapters that follow. I argue that male sexual violence—envisioned in fantasy and enacted against women—has roots in a culture of manhood that reaches from sea to shining sea, with historical sources in our early national period. Our cultural addiction to sexual violence is knotted into the American Dream, entangled with ideals of independence, equality, and self-reliance that make us proud to be Americans. How could anything so furtive as pornography, or as patently illegal as rape and spousal abuse, be married to admirable and widely celebrated ideals? The short answer is that these abuses are justified through a perversion of the democratic ideal, the doctrine of equal rights twisted to defend a regime that violates the sexual autonomy of women. Yet hidden behind this simple contradiction is a dense web of psychosocial forces that gives sexual violence its power to enthrall the imaginations of men and to perpetuate itself as an element of American manhood.

By showing that contemporary patterns of sexual violence have been built up over time, I hope to aid in the effort to dismantle the pornographic enchantments that guide and enable it. Not that violent pornography leads to rape in some lockstep causal sequence, but that both pornography and sexually abusive conduct arise from chronic dilemmas of male gendering.

Stemming from a shared source, the interplay between pornography and sexual violence is complex and various; but my attention here focuses on the source, a pattern of masculinity that received its distinctive American form in the late eighteenth century and has unfolded historically since. This argument explicitly refutes the claim that sexual violence is "natural," meaning that it is determined by genetically hard-wired biological imperatives. Dispelling the mythology of "natural" male violence, and demonstrating the historical conditions in which it acquired its present form, so I hope and believe, will enlarge the resources available to those who seek justice in the intimate relations of women and men.

The epilogue will return to my personal experience, to retell the story of the Waldo train station as I now understand it, as I continue to seek liberation from the cultural legacy I found within myself as boyhood came to an end. Opening new horizons of gender, in which men find sexual intimacy with women on equal terms, requires understanding that legacy, seeing how it harms our personal relationships, and learning to transcend it. We must break the tradition of sexually violent manhood and apply the ideal of equality to our intimate lives, shaping manhoods and womanhoods in its light.

1

Frontiers of Masculinity

SEXUAL VIOLENCE is a core issue of feminist literary and social criticism. Kate Millett's *Sexual Politics* (1970) and Susan Brownmiller's *Against Our Will: Men, Women and Rape* (1975) inaugurated the contemporary discussion concerning rape, pornography, and domestic violence, which has shown that sexual victimization is inherent to the situation of women in male-dominant social arrangements. Yet while sexual violence enforces the domination of men over women, it also has powerful hidden sources in the relations of men with men and men with themselves. Diana Scully's study of convicted rapists led her to declare, in *Understanding Sexual Violence* (1990), that such abuse is a male problem and should be addressed by men prepared to accept responsibility for tracing its origins in the lives men lead.

In 1979 Paul Kivel co-founded the Oakland Men's Project to carry forward "men's work," the effort of men to reconsider boys' socialization into manhood and to undo the ingrained patterns that prompt violence against women. The anti-rape activists Timothy Beneke and John Stoltenberg likewise pioneered efforts on this frontier in the 1980s, as did Joseph Pleck, whose *The Myth of Masculinity* (1981) created a new curriculum of sociological study. There also now exists a substantial body of work by psychologists that treats sexual violence as endemic to a form of manhood that is instilled in growing boys.[1] Programs of intervention for wife batterers and sex offenders, like recent approaches to the rearing of boys and new psychotherapies for adult men, incorporate the recognition that men are trained to protect a "mask of masculinity" that conceals a troubled human face (Pollack, *Real Boys* 3–19; Real 1–19).

This present-day style of manhood arose from an historical tradition whose development can be traced in works of American literature, and the effort to build more humane forms of masculinity in our own time can be aided by an understanding of that tradition. Our gendered selves are not dictated by biology, nor are they happenstance constructions that can be reconstructed at will: they are historical institutions. The social landscape that we now inhabit has been shaped by slow-moving processes that reach deep into the past.

It is now apparent that sexual violence is akin to other manhood-reinforcing forms of abuse. Homophobia, wife battering, and child abuse also have sources in the core anxieties of an internally contradictory manhood. The tradition that instills this incoherent and unstable role provides a man with traditional ways of compensating for its chronic distresses. Gay men, children, and women become gender scapegoats; they are seen to embody what the man finds "unmanly" in himself. Punishing them temporarily fends off anxieties by confirming the illusion that the man's troubles come from others, not from within himself. Because sexual desire is among the forces threatening such masculinity, compensatory violence enters sexual relations; and conversely, wife beating, homophobic assault, and child abuse frequently carry an erotic tinge. Rape and sexual harassment are only the most overt forms of the sexual violence whose origins I seek to trace.

Much of the current literature on reconstructing masculinity rejects "male bashing," and asks for an "empathic" approach to the maladies men suffer because of the gender straitjacket in which we find ourselves confined.[2] Yet chronically anxious men, Bryce Traister has recently noted, wield formidable social power over women. On the issue of sexual abuse, in particular, empathy must collaborate with its apparent opposite, a policy of resolute prohibition, and with a determined effort to correct the unjust social arrangements that encourage and protect offenders. We badly need more extensive and demanding legal prohibitions against domestic violence and sexual coercion, and the enforcement of current law needs to be strengthened.

This book explains the historically conditioned dilemmas that prompt men to commit sexual offenses, but does not extenuate them. As things now stand, men are right to expect that committing rape and sexual harassment will carry scant penalty, if any. Offenders anticipate that answerable officials—in business, the professions, the military, and institutions of higher education—will extend them *post facto* permission, as will police, attorneys, judges, and juries. Stephen Schulhofer, in *Unwanted Sex,* abundantly documents the inadequate state of current law on issues of rape and sexual harassment and makes suggestions for a major overhaul. Better law and more stringent enforcement should help bring men to their senses, to confront the sexually abusive impulses they are now permitted to act out.

Women and men alike have strong motives—though different ones—for shunning these issues. The sexual abuse women suffer imposes on them a cost that is largely invisible to men. In *The Female Fear*, Margaret Gordon and Stephanie Riger report that more than eighty percent of women fear for their safety to a degree that substantially impairs their freedom of movement (cited in Schulhofer 49). A subsurface reservoir of terror prevents women from leaving the house alone in the evening, from entering clubs alone, from walking alone in their neighborhoods, from going to the movies after dark. This produces an equally large subsurface reservoir of rage.

Men too have their secret hysteria, a desperation and guilt connected with the tacit recognition that women face intolerable sexual oppression, that men are answerable for it, yet that rooting out its sources seems impossible. Many men contemptuously brush aside feminist protests against sexual exploitation, or parry them with jokes; but few men assert male privilege directly. We do not claim explicitly that our manhood entitles us to indulge in coercive sex. The lip service that is paid to sexual justice often works to facilitate unjust conduct, but it also bespeaks an uneasy male conscience. Most men find fantasy scenarios of sexual coercion to be sexually stimulating, and thus find within themselves impulses of the sort that are acted out in offenses against women. Yet such impulses are notably tenacious, arising as they do from long-standing social arrangements. Until means are found to understand and to remedy the masculine proclivity for sexual abuse, men have only their helpless shame to offer in response to the helpless rage of women.

Strategies of denial have strong appeal when we are bedeviled by irresolvable distresses, so we find it plausible that sexual abuse is committed by an aberrant minority of men, and that broad-scale patterns of social injustice that reach into the lives of male newborns, and guide them through boyhood into manhood, have nothing to do with it. Confronting the sexually violent disposition instilled by our received tradition of manhood is likely to arouse phobic responses in women and men alike. Yet we must brave those responses if we are to envision democratic masculinities worthy of the name and to chart a pathway toward their realization.

I argue that there are distinct historical traditions of American masculinity, and that prominent among these is a despotic manhood at odds with democratic principle, whose psychosocial requirements promote the sexual violation of women. This style of manliness descends from a tradition of warrior manhood that existed in varying forms long before the United States came into being, and when we come to analyze its American version we will see that it poorly serves the actual needs of American warriors. But it supports nonetheless a culture of sexual coercion.[3]

During the 1996 presidential campaign, Bob Dole denounced sex and violence in the media. When asked for the title of a movie he admired, Dole mentioned *True Lies*, an adventure flick starring Arnold Schwarzenegger and Jamie Lee Curtis (Goldstein 118). The film culminates in a display of licit ultraviolence, as Schwarzenegger massacres a horde of third-world figures. The film also offers a display of licit sexual coercion.

Curtis plays an airhead suburbanite who is unaware that her husband (Schwarzenegger) is a secret agent. Bored by his pantomime of bland normality, she starts a flirtation with a man who pretends to be a spy. When Schwarzenegger suspects she's having an affair, he kidnaps her and places her alone in a huge featureless interrogation room at his government headquarters. There a loudspeaker voice convinces her that her husband will be killed unless she has sex with a stranger. The payoff sequence begins when Curtis arrives at the appointed hotel room, where the lighting is arranged to conceal the "stranger's" face, so that she doesn't see it's Schwarzenegger himself. Her face a mask of loathing, Curtis performs an elaborate striptease, writhing and twisting to gratify the man in the shadows.

If a woman paid out money because she was terrified by a false threat to her husband's life, the transaction would count as fraud under current legal definitions. It would violate her property rights. But the law recognizes no such right over providing erotic gratification. No actionable offense would have occurred in this scenario, even if the woman had submitted to sexual intercourse (as Curtis does not), and even if the woman and man had not been married (Schulhofer 139–159). In the film, likewise, this clear instance of sexual abuse brings no discredit on the husband. That he and his wife might have had an honest conversation about their marital unhappiness is unthinkable within the axioms of the genre. On the contrary, the key to their romantic revitalization is sexual coercion, which enhances the titillation that Curtis's striptease provides its viewers. In *True Lies* Schwarzenegger is an American patriot whose manly heroism incorporates the sexual abuse of women.

Yet American gender traditions also include alternative possibilities for men, and the American context provides ideological sources for an attack on despotic manhood and the sexual violence it entails. The ideal of equality was extended only gradually beyond white men to include black men, and only in the twentieth century did women gain the exercise of their right to vote. This democratic ideal is now reaching into the bed-and-board frontier, the intimate relations of women and men, where women's sexual autonomy must be recognized as an inherent right. Sexually coercive masculinity, like race hatred, not only violates its immediate victims; it also violates the true meaning of American democracy. The psychic protocols of despotic manhood, as we shall see, leave men scarcely able to conceptualize (much less act upon) relationships of equality, not only with women also with other men.

It may seem strange to say that abusive sexuality arises from a disposition that has a history, indeed an American history, or that there now exists a "frontier" on which change is possible. Are not rage and desire—the motives for rape—primordial emotions that lie beyond the reach of historical processes?

Sigmund Freud and Carl Jung inaugurated traditions of psychoanalytic study that seek to describe fixed inborn mental structures and the vicissitudes of their development. These pioneers disagreed on many points, but both claimed access to presumptively timeless universals of psychic life. Pressed to its limits, this axiom yields silly results, implying that the sexualities of ancient Greeks, Reformation clergy, and nineteenth-century Kentucky frontiersmen are identical, and that contemporary neuroses in Berkeley, Yokohama, and Buenos Aires all require the same routines of diagnosis and treatment.

Literary and historical scholars are beginning to avail themselves of an alternative tradition that examines the social constitution of psychological structures. Recent developments in neuroscience indicate that psychic worlds are constructed as the brains of infants develop. Humans are born with constructive capacities, it now appears, but with minimal fixed plans. The impulse to find or make meaning may be a human universal, but the systems of meaning that pattern our psychosocial lives are not.[4] Psychic structures live in history. They take form like other cultural institutions, undergo changes, compete with alternative institutions, and eventually pass from the scene. Thus opens a new vista of study, a paleopsychology that pursues the historical understanding of earlier selfhoods, not the Freudian or Jungian decoding of them. Current psychic arrangements—those which operate so powerfully within us, and in the society around us—likewise become susceptible to historical investigation.

Still, male sexual violence may seem to stand apart from such complexities. Is not violent aggression, including sexual aggression, genetically innate to males? Is it not readily visible in diverse cultures and historical epochs, as well as in nonhuman species? In *Demonic Males*—a study of our primate cousins—Richard Wrangham and Dale Peterson report that chimpanzees carry out lethal search-and-destroy missions against rival groups, and that male chimps sometimes force females to copulate. Among orangutans rape is not incidental; it is the routine means of sexual congress for males who lack the capacity to acquire a harem (132–141). Male humans throughout history have forced women into sex, sometimes collectively, as in the slaveholding South, the enforced prostitution of Jewish and Korean captives during World War II, and the horrors of contemporary Bosnia. Single men, rather than couples, were sent by the Spanish crown to colonize Mexico, with the expectation that they would populate the imperial colony by means of native women obtained through conquest.

It does not follow, however, that sexual violence is universal across human cultures, everywhere carried out in accordance with uniform genetic instructions. As I've talked with male colleagues and friends about this book, all have acknowledged their awareness of the widespread male fascination with sexual violence; but some have added that they themselves do not share in it. Even making generous allowances for repression and denial, I've concluded that such claims are often quite truthful. Some men simply do not experience such responses; yet they surely possess a full complement of male genes. American men grow up in distinct ethnicities, are reared in distinctive familial microcultures, with differing social histories and differing legacies of psychic strength and liability. The anthropological research of Peggy Reeves Sanday and David Gilmore confirms the role of culture here, showing that the incidence of rape varies markedly among human societies rather than standing apart as a genetic constant.

Even when a pattern of social relations is historically commonplace, it does not follow that the genetic code immutably decrees it. Efforts to abolish American slavery will fail, said its nineteenth-century defenders, because history and the Bible—like contemporary cultures around the world—demonstrate that slavery is dictated by human nature.

There is reason to believe that male primates, including humans, may share a genetic proclivity to kill the offspring of their mates when those offspring are fathered by other males. Wrangham and Peterson observe that infant gorillas and chimpanzees are at risk from infanticidal adult males, and that females adopt differing strategies to reduce the risk. Female gorillas attach themselves to powerful silverbacks to protect their young. Female chimps mate with as many males as possible so as to confuse the question of which male was the sire.

Among lions infanticide is notably prompt; when a younger male carries out a "takeover," ousting an older male from control of the pride and taking the females as mates, he immediately kills off the cubs, clearing the way for his own offspring

(Wrangham and Peterson 146-158). Human stepparents are substantially more likely to abuse and murder children in the household than are biological parents. But there is no social permission—tacit or otherwise—to excuse these crimes on the ground that they are "natural."[5]

Exactly such social permission exists in abundance for rape and spousal abuse, deriving from the belief that sexual violence is inherent in the nature of men. The same permission applies in cases of sexual murder: we respond to a stepfather's infanticide with unqualified horror, but when a woman is killed in the course of rape or spousal abuse, we're inclined to think that a regrettably understandable situation somehow got out of hand. Or we decide that it's a case of "domestic violence," something native to family life, where women have primary responsibility for maintaining affectionate relationships.

The sexual pressures within men feel primordial—and thus determined by biological imperatives—because we have inherited a cultural tradition telling us they are. A pernicious morality follows: that a sexually aroused man is not answerable for complying with the dictates of his genetic constitution, and that responsibility for male sexual aggression belongs to the woman, particularly if she can be imagined to have aroused him intentionally.

Our erotic experience, as we live it vividly moment by moment, is not constructed out of nothing. Sexuality—like eating, speaking, and dying—is grounded in genetic capabilities and imperatives. But we know our sexuality, and live it out, as a cultural institution, which we have inherited from the past.

The term "intercourse" now most often refers to sexual relations; but before about 1820, according to the *Oxford English Dictionary*, the term belonged to commerce and diplomacy. "Intercourse" envisions coition as an interaction between persons who—like nations and corporations—bring distinct identities to the exchange. It is a communicative act, a language of tactile pleasure through which persons convey their mutual knowledge and affection. This complex of meanings was established in the early nineteenth century by an emerging ideal of marriage that placed the intimate union of the two partners at the center of the institution, and it strongly implies that intercourse is valid only when both parties consent. Before the emergence of this marital ideal—as a union of freely contracting partners—the concept of marital rape was virtually unimaginable.

To glimpse the historical relation of sexual violence and warrior manhood, consider the history of "pussy." The squeamishness imputed to cats made the term suitable for execrating cowardly men long before it acquired its contemporary misogynist significance. Lady Macbeth's gender-shaming tirade scolds her husband for shilly-shallying like "the poor cat i' the adage," instead of acting like a "man" (1.7.44). The *OED* gives an 1847 citation describing soldiers as "too pussy" to put up a fight. Uses of the term to demean women and homosexuals came later.

When a drill sergeant calls recruits "pussies," he ostensibly invokes a degraded form of womanhood in order to shame young men into a fighting spirit. But the semantic history of the term suggests a logic running in the opposite direction: "pussy" is the nausea men feel at the prospect of killing and being killed. Women are conscripted into the business of marking that nausea as contemptible. The qualities of a stigmatized manhood—including admirable qualities—lie at the core of the meaning.

Charting the frontiers across which sexually violent manhood has developed in America can be aided by the study of literary art, because literature gives access to the textures of intimate experience. Nothing survives from the human past that registers more fully the psychosocial conflicts that haunted our forebears and the imaginative transactions by which they sought to make sense of their lives. Literature gives us more than theories about human experience; it gives us an imitation of experience itself, on terms that free us from practical responsibility. As readers we share in feelings vicariously, respond to circumstances for which we are not answerable, follow lines of reasoning for fun, and are thus freed to commune directly with the ordering of emotion, circumstance, and thought. When they attain significant cultural power, literary works engage the structural principles by which we make sense of our lives, including the principles that guide us, or misguide us, in living as women and men.

Sexual violence is rightly the province of criminologists, evolutionary biologists, anthropologists, paleohistorians, psychologists, sociologists, political historians, self-help and mental health scholars, and counselors to victims of sexual abuse, as well as counselors to the men who commit these offenses. Yet writing in these fields relies, at luminous critical moments, on narrative. My reading has led me to arresting stories across a diverse range: of criminal profiling, of manhood rituals among the !Kung, of successful Boston businessmen contemplating suicide, of chimpanzee rape. Such anecdotes, well chosen and well told, are not mere window dressing; they have notable analytic power, making palpable the dynamic interplay of intangible things like gender systems. Robert Coles recently commented that novelists, making no claim to science, offer sophisticated analyses of the way boys grow into men.

Powerful works of literature—*The Scarlet Letter, Uncle Tom's Cabin, The Red Badge of Courage, A Farewell to Arms, Native Son*—portray dilemmas of American masculinity in the forms given by successive historical epochs, even as they speak directly to readers in our own generation. The developing political, economic, and cultural institutions that have shaped sexually violent manhood—capitalism, marriage, law, slavery, war, race hatred, American democracy—find their way into the unfolding story of literary art. The literature we've inherited illuminates the selves we've inherited, dramatizing the conflicted traditions that our society trains us to make our own. The pathologies of contemporary American manhood continue to roil and torment our lives in patterns that have been discernable since the tradition took root in the early national period, when the intuitions of literary artists began to search them out.

Literary criticism is devoted here to an ethical project, that of examining the symbolic structures that go into the making of men, and of permitting us to see through and correct the injustices of a prevalent way of being masculine. This enterprise belongs to a tradition that students of American literature pioneered in the mid-twentieth century. Henry Nash Smith published *Virgin Land* in 1950, followed by R. W. B. Lewis, *The American Adam* (1955); Leslie A. Fiedler, *Love and Death in the American Novel* (1960); and Leo Marx, *The Machine in the Garden* (1964).

This "myth and symbol" school framed the curriculum of American literary studies that developed after World War II, defining persistent features of an American self by reviewing a procession of classic literary works. We now have more sophisticated understandings of "myth and symbol"—grounded in social psychology, neo-Marxism and interpretive anthropology—that permit us to study the historical changes through which cultural systems pass and the changing identities they sponsor. Feminist criticism, postcolonial studies, and African-American studies have produced a body of ethical analysis that is compelling not because it propounds moral rules but because it sheds light on the unfolding traditions of selfhood that make and break rules.

Yet even in these areas literary study has become increasingly sequestered, as monographs proliferate to meet the demands of tenure. American literature at large is too often embraced and defined by market-share anthologies, and literary scholarship proves relevant to intricate cognitive proceedings that begin and end in the classroom, not to what happens in people's lives, to say nothing of sexual abuse on campus.

In this book I attempt no comprehensive discussion of the American story, within which there are multiple ethnic variations, nor do I offer a fully nuanced treatment of the relevant historical contexts. I seek instead to track the moving frontier by identifying its major landmarks, at which shifts in social and economic conditions alter the terms on which abusive male sexuality is perpetuated and challenged.

The tradition perpetuating male supremacy in America has been accompanied by a counter-tradition seeking reforms that recognize the equality of women with men. This struggle for democratic principle has focused on securing economic and political rights, but has included from the outset a demand for justice within intimate relationships. Today fierce public debates are taking place at the bed-and-board frontier, where the textures of personal selfhood are undergoing change. Sexuality and gender identity are no longer seen as immutable givens: manhoods can be reshaped to promise a greater measure of truthfulness, justice, and love in relationships between women and men. In this sharply polarized scene, the loudest partisans are promoting the traditional malady, but others are at work creating new forms of democratic masculinity.

2

Rape as an Activity of the Imagination

WALT WHITMAN ARDENTLY championed the democratic ideal. His poetry repeatedly affirms that no social elite—whether bloodline gentry, slaveowners, or capitalist proprietors—can legitimately direct the lives of ordinary women and men without their consent; and he dedicated his life to the poetic celebration of this creed in defiance of restrictive social conventions. Whitman's democratic vision and his creative independence remain inspiring today, not least because his poetic celebration of same-sex desire—which made him a pariah in his own time—continues to assist gay men and women in the quest for self-affirmation.[1]

In "A Woman Waits for Me" Whitman offers himself, soul and body, as a living incarnation of democracy, in which women fulfill their sexual capacities equally with men.

> Without shame the man I like knows and avows the
>   deliciousness of his sex,
> Without shame the woman I like knows and avows hers.

Such women are independent and self-reliant; they "know how to swim, row, ride, wrestle, shoot, run, strike, retreat, advance, resist, defend themselves." "A Woman Waits for Me" has been anthologized as a landmark in the quest for sexual equality, distinguishing Whitman as a rare pro-feminist male voice, honoring women who "are ultimate in their own right . . . calm, clear, well possess'd of themselves" (Kimmel and Mosmiller 299).

Yet such women fulfill their democratic womanhood, and Whitman fulfills his democratic manhood, when he rapes them.

> It is I, you women, I make my way,
> I am stern, acrid, large, undissuadable, but I love you,
> I do not hurt you any more than is necessary for you,
> I pour the stuff to start sons and daughters fit for these
>   States, I press with slow rude muscle,
> I brace myself effectually, I listen to no entreaties,
> I dare not withdraw until I deposit what has so long
>   accumulated within me.

Whitman proclaims that the true sons and daughters of American democracy are engendered in rape and are destined for rape. Their womanhood and manhood will be defined in endless replications of this moment, in which the woman is hurt (only as "necessary") when the man penetrates her in defiance of her entreaties.[2]

The woman is two opposite things simultaneously: she is sexually self-possessed *and* she finds fulfillment when forced into sexual intercourse. These contradictory realities are fused into a seamless plausible anecdote by the imaginative structures defining manhood and womanhood for the audience Whitman addressed. Whitman did not invent this paradox, but he articulates it with consummate accuracy, especially in connecting the doublethink about women with ideals of democracy and natural manhood.

In subsequent chapters we will investigate Whitman's paradox in its historical context; here we lay open the anatomy of the core fantasy as it remains in force today. We must trace the illogic that holds women to possess and not possess moral autonomy in sexual matters and leads men to assume that rape is and is not rape.

Beginning in the late 1970s the FBI's Behavioral Sciences Unit pioneered the comparative study of sex-crime scenes and found that they fall into discernable categories, conforming to profiles by which groups of offenders may be classed. As organized crime scenes differ from disorganized, so "power assurance rapists" differ from "anger rapists," who differ from "sadists." Every crime scene possesses a "signature" that indicates something of the personal meaning that the rape held for the offender. Psychological studies of convicted rapists, in turn, have cast light on the underlying logic that binds these meanings together.

Rapists share an imaginative life marked by intrusive fantasies of sexual assault, a preoccupation typically beginning in boyhood that flourishes in puberty and that is sustained through pornography long before the offender commits his first rape. Crime scenes indicate the character of such fantasies and the state of their development. "Disorganized" scenes are created by men who obey the impulse to enact the fantasy without forethought, in the midst of disorienting anxieties, or whose rage prompts them to make a "blitz" attack. Objects stolen from victims also play a role, serving as souvenirs through which the rapist can trigger retrospective fantasies of the event.

"Organized" rapists sometimes elaborate their fantasies through precursory activities as well. Ann Burgess and her associates discuss a multiple offender who saw one of his victims out shopping some months after the assault and recognized her plaid dress. She had not been wearing the dress at the time of the attack, but it appeared in family photographs that he had examined on the numerous occasions when he had entered her apartment and familiarized himself with her belongings. He had embellished his fantasy with details drawn from the victim's life, said the rapist, so she would not be "a stranger" (292).

Yet the victim was all the more a stranger because of the information the rapist had collected. His knowledge of her may have been accurate, but it was organized exclusively by his own needs. The feminist critique of male perspectives in business, politics, and academic research can be applied without revision to his investigations. The victim's daily life was known to him, but told him nothing of her personal reality. Like Whitman's victim, the woman ceased to exist as a person in her own right, even as the man lavished attention on her.

Sexual crimes are an activity of the imagination; they are committed in order to cultivate and sustain fantasies that take part in, and contribute to, long-standing cultural myths. Not all men who have fantasies of sexual violence commit sexual crimes, and why certain men cross the line into enactment is not well understood.[3] Yet it is clear that rapist fantasies capture the imaginations of law-abiding men.

Fantasies of sexual violence are a staple of the symbolic diet that sustains the popular imagination, not least in the media. Helen Benedict quotes a reporter for the *New York Post* who was listening to the police radio when the murder of eighteen-year-old Jennifer Levin was first called in: "We heard the words 'Central Park, young white teenager, gorgeous, and strangled' . . . It was sex, tits and ass, and a strangling—we knew it would sell" (147). The Levin case sold very well; it provided material for three years of newspaper articles and television reports. News-media porn is mild and sparse compared to the provender available in popular novels and film. Grocery stores have book-displays with covers that feature women wriggling in the grasp of shirtless men, and in the movies Rhett Butler is still kicking down the bedroom door, to say nothing of the sexual aggression in X-rated films. Sexual coercion is portrayed as normal, even as amusing, in a wide range of popular entertainments; as Deborah Rhode relates, more than a third of the sexual exchanges in television comedies "meet the legal definition of harassment" (83).

The exploits of famous criminals become legendary, taking on an imaginative life of their own. Henry Lee Lucas is now well established in the folklore of serial rape and murder, if not so famous as Jack the Ripper, the Boston Strangler, or Ted Bundy. With his slashed eye, his slack mouth, and his hooked nose shadowing a scruffy beard, Lucas evoked the sex-murderer as redneck, a monster from Dogpatch. In this irresistible bit of media theatre, the fiend escapes his southern gothic lair to roam the impersonal freeways of an urbanized America, leaving a trail of ravished corpses in his wake. Following his arrest in 1982, the public eagerly consumed Lucas's confessions, which mounted from dozens to scores to hundreds.

Lucas did not invent all the particulars of the crimes to which he confessed; it seems that law enforcement officials were caught up in the excitement and more or less consciously gave him details of murders to be recycled in his confessions. Unlike O. J. Simpson, Lucas did not bring celebrity status to the media frenzy that surrounded him; he generated his myth on the spot by exploiting the popular infatuation with stories of sexual murder. Before sobriety prevailed, Lucas became a marketable commodity, and he remained so after his fanciful confessions were exposed. An instant biography was produced, with a cassette recording of selected confessions, followed by the film *Henry, Portrait of a Serial Killer,* which quickly became available on video, as did the follow-up, *Henry 2.*

Of course the Lucas case testifies to our collective abhorrence for sexual violence; the apparatus of law enforcement—the police, the courts, and the prison system—was called into play. But the pornographic fascination that filled the media and qualified the work of law enforcement testifies to the continued vitality of Whitman's paradox. "Orange Socks" symbolizes the obliteration of women's reality in the male fantasies that generated the Lucas legend. "Orange Socks" is the single case on which Lucas was convicted, and the term designates a victim whose identity remains unknown. As the news media never tire of repeating, she was given the nickname because her body was naked when it was discovered, except for the socks.

For women, rape is a horrible experience. Recovery may take months or years, and is rarely completed. Previously satisfying sexual relationships are often devastated, and the victim is besieged by post-traumatic stress in the form of intrusive memories of abuse accompanied by periods of disabling anxiety. Victims sometimes make drastic alterations in their life patterns—changing jobs, moving to a new residence, dropping out of school—in order to remove themselves from circumstances that recall the trauma. Therapeutic literature recommends that rape victims, like victims of child abuse, define themselves as "survivors," so as to take command of their torments psychologically. But this laudable strategy should not blur awareness that raped women are surviving an atrocity.

Male fantasies of rape leave out this nightmare. Comparative studies have shown that men and woman alike are sexually aroused by films of petting and sexual intercourse, and are particularly aroused by depictions of orgasm, including involuntary orgasms experienced by women as a consequence of male sexual aggression. But men and women differ sharply when the victim of aggression suffers pain: men show high levels of arousal at such scenarios; women do not (Scully 152).

Except for the very small population of overt sadists, sexual offenders subscribe to a delusionary picture of their victims' experience. According to the work of Diana Scully, rapists typically believe that their victims more or less covertly invited the attack, either by dress or by provocative conduct. Rapists also report that after an initial pseudo-resistance their victims experienced the rape as pleasurable. Rapists sometimes claim that the assault exposes a woman's hypocrisy, that she assumes a false mantle of innocence and virtue, but that her conduct during the rape reveals that she yearns for it, and that she is actually "very experienced." The rapist sometimes imagines that his victim discovered desires she had kept secret from herself, and that his attack struck home to her inner truth. Some of the rapists in Scully's sample insisted that they had fulfilled *their victims'* fantasies.[4]

Where do these stunning delusions originate? Studies of male-on-male rape demonstrate that victims experience trauma and post-traumatic suffering virtually indistinguishable from that suffered by women—the whole complement of anxiety attacks, intrusive memories, runaway terror and rage, and disrupted sexuality (Groth and Birnbaum 133–141). Scully notes that men who rape women invoke a distorted picture of their victim's experience in order to escape responsibility and shift blame onto the victim. Yet this maneuver would not work if the popular myth were not firmly ensconced in the sexual responses of men who are not rapists. The rapist's fantasy becomes plausible to police investigators, prosecutors, judges, juries, and the press because those law-abiding parties share in it and believe in the distorted picture of reality it offers.

Rapists themselves subscribe to the myth. It is possible that certain offenders recount tales of the victim's covert initiative and pleasure in contradiction to their own actual recollections, cynically appealing to a popular fantasy they know to be false. But in the main, I propose, such accounts are candid, and explaining them requires an analysis that looks beyond the benefits of conscious deceit. Rape fantasies are produced by an imaginative activity that conceals its own traces: men chronically inhabit a delusional subjective reality in which they are teased by sexually provocative women who pretend to lack sexual desire, only to reveal it once assaulted.

Where does this delusion come from? How does it acquire such power? Why do men project it onto the experience of raped women, in defiance of the trauma women undergo, and equally in defiance of the male experience of being raped? What is the male investment in this fantasy? Such pornographic enchantment manifestly contributes to the male permissiveness that blocks collective action against sexual violence. But how did it get to be so tenacious?

An important answer holds that the myth serves male dominance, as rape itself does. Susan Brownmiller pioneered the tradition of feminist study demonstrating that the dread of sexual assault limits the physical mobility of women, restricts their occupational opportunities, hampers their exercise of political rights, and injures their psychic well-being. Rapists make women dependent for protection on men: boyfriends, husbands, brothers, and male law enforcement officers. A tacit collusion keeps rape alive in order to maintain the male protection racket, encouraging and excusing offenders even as they are tracked down and punished. The rape myth supports this collusion.

Still, politically useful falsehoods come and go, while delusions about rape are peculiarly resistant to debunking. In *Virgin or Vamp*, her 1992 study of sex crimes in the media, Helen Benedict found that two decades of intensive criticism and public exposure had failed to discredit the myth, or to reduce its influence in newspaper and television reporting (13). Other fantasies sustaining male dominance, by contrast, have collapsed. It was believed in the nineteenth century that women who attended college would lose their physical vitality and their capacity for motherhood, but the experience of female college graduates quickly demolished that myth. We now have no popular literature featuring women incapacitated by acquiring a Phi Beta Kappa key at Harvard. Yet the testimony of rape victims, in far greater volume, tells little against the rape myth. Why?

Return to Whitman's poem for a moment to notice the grandiosity of the speaking voice:

> It is I, you women, I make my way
> I am stern, acrid, large, undissuadable, but I love you,
> I do not hurt you any more than is necessary for you,

I pour the stuff to start sons and daughters fit for these
    States, I press with slow rude muscle,
I brace myself effectually, I listen to no entreaties,
I dare not withdraw till I deposit what has so long
    accumulated within me.

These lines project an all-encompassing manhood, fully in command of itself as it takes command of the woman, and confidently envisioning the destined offspring. Whitman's penis is a "muscle," subject to exact control, like the thighs and hips that brace its unhurried pressure.

A clue to the male psychology that sustains the rape myth lies in the inflated bravado of Whitman's voice, which speaks against an obscure yet insistent voice of opposition. His grandiosity works to counteract an implied resistance, a distress that lurks beneath the surface of the poem. What unspoken tremor is Whitman shouting down?

Whitman pictures the rape as a relief of his sexual frustration, and this contributes to the larger drama he envisions. The matched genders—male and female—form a sexual conjunction that accommodates his concealed anxiety. As Whitman seeks to "brace" himself against the "entreaties" of the woman, he braces himself against himself. The woman who waits for him, perfectly suited to him, is a proxy for something within Whitman.

This poem articulates a conflicted masculine psychology that had become current when Whitman published it in 1856 and remains alive today. The rape myth, then and now, supplants the actual experience of men with a fantasy in which "you women" are made to embody perplexities that men seek to hold at bay.

Thoreau's *Walden*, published two years earlier, gave classic expression to the male predicament that is hidden within fantasies of dominating women sexually: "the mass of men lead lives of quiet desperation." In his cabin by the pond, Thoreau contemplated the distress that an emerging economic order had built into men's lives: "Always promising to pay, promising to pay, tomorrow, and dying to-day insolvent; seeking to curry favor, to get custom . . . contracting yourself into a nutshell of civility, or dilating into an atmosphere of thin and vaporous generosity, that you may persuade your neighbor to let you make his shoes, or his hat, or his coat, or his carriage, or import his groceries for him" (3-4). A new ethos of ceaseless economic competition not only instills desperation but requires men to keep quiet about it, and thus to seek no remedy for it. Thoreau declares that the resultant hopelessness shapes the social landscape: "A stereotyped but unconscious despair is concealed even under what are called the games and amusements of mankind" (4-5).

There is a bedrock connection between Whitman's rapist manhood and Thoreau's collective stifled panic, which provides historical grounding for the rape myth that remains compelling in our own time. The fantasies of sexual violation that grip the imaginations of men are—like Thoreau's "games and amusements"—unavailing efforts to forestall or escape covert desperation. Substantiating this sketchy historical claim will occupy the better part of the next two chapters; the psychological structure at work requires further attention now.

A company of sociologists and psychologists—including Gary Brooks, Ronald Levant, David Lisak, Joseph Pleck, and William Pollack—analyze manhood as a socially conditioned role that possesses built-in liabilities. Their work has shown that the traditional male role is traumatic for boys entering the process of socialization and entails humiliation and perplexity throughout a man's life.

Boy babies, it turns out, are more emotionally expressive than girls; they show delight and irritation more readily, and they cry more. But boys are trained through systematic shaming and rebuffs to bottle up their distresses and their joys, and by the age of six they are far more inhibited than their more emotionally confident sisters. The early attack on the emotional vitality of boys bequeaths a familiar set of troubles. Adult men find their intimate relationships blighted by emotional dilemmas they can scarcely discern in themselves. Afflicted by a craving for emotional comfort that is crosscut by resentment, they demand compensation in the here and now for the traumas of boyhood (Levant, "Nonrelational" 16, 21).

The classic pattern of traditional manhood demands an impossible performance of self-reliance and self-command. Men test their manly mettle in competitions against other men, in which there are always more losers than winners; and even winners are subject to the uncontrollable mischances of living.

American men are not exempted from the tragic limitations and vulnerabilities of human experience generally, yet the code of masculine toughness requires denying their reality. It is impossible to maintain stoic composure—to "take it like a man"—when distress is overwhelming, so that a compulsively self-reliant man refuses to believe that overwhelming distress can ever befall him. He cannot afford to acknowledge what everyman suffers: the contingencies of his economic fate, his need for intimate companionship, his exposure to illness, to emotional tumult, to accident and misfortune. However strenuously banished from consciousness, these realities continue to exert pressure on his psychic life.

The result is a contemporary version of Thoreau's "quiet desperation," which Terrence Real terms "covert depression." Men suffer this affliction when they cannot recognize their ingrained distresses as part of the self because early boyhood shaming has become an unconscious inner mechanism. The male self is not merely split between "manly" and "unmanly" segments: covert depression is inner warfare, a chronic self-assault that Real likens to an autoimmune disease (54).[5]

The body's immune system maintains a sharp distinction between the "self" and the "not self," so that alien invaders—viruses, bacteria, splinters—are identified as antigens, and the system designs antibodies to attack them. In diseases like lupus, the system goes awry and the body makes war on itself, mistaking its own tissues for the enemy. The thoughts and feelings of men that cannot be reconciled to self-command are marked as "not self" and are defined as targets for attack, not with biological agents but with psychic weapons custom-tailored for the occasion—abhorrence, ridicule, contempt, and loathing.

Sexual desire is among the subversive experiences that disconcert masculine self-command and thus menace masculine self-respect. Sexual yearnings place a man at another person's disposal, subject to that person's impulses and decisions. Michael Warner has noted that gay men become targets of phobic hatred not only because they desire other men but because they *desire;* same-sex preference calls attention to a disquieting fact, namely that they are sexual men. The politics of sexual shame traps heterosexual men as well, especially if their lives suggest a sexuality not wholly under voluntary command (*Trouble* 17–40). Men vigilant to refuse the inner experience of sexual abjection seek unilateral control in sexual relations, which in its milder form is a male monopoly on the initiation of sexual encounters and their direction once initiated. When unilateral control becomes coercion, as in Whitman's poem, it's rape. Sexual intercourse also poses the prospect of interpersonal closeness, which autoimmune men perceive as a danger to their autonomy.

Students of contemporary masculinity have noted the prevalence of a "nonrelational" sexuality in which sexual intimacy is divorced from emotional intimacy. The "centerfold syndrome" is an example of this: men caught up in a persistent fantasy life that feeds on images of women with whom they will never exchange a word, while they feel sexually awkward with actual women who love them. Traditional manhood encourages men to be aggressive, moreover, and to funnel emotions of vulnerability and neediness into anger, and this syndrome can generate a sexuality in which coercion is routine (Brooks, "Centerfold"; Levant, "Nonrelational"). Gary Brooks and L. B. Silverstein argue that the "dark side" of masculinity—including violence against women in the family, rape and sexual assault, sexual harassment in the workplace—is not a problem of aberrant men who have somehow failed to fulfill the conventional role. On the contrary, such pathologies represent hypermasculinity, the accentuation of traits entailed by manhood as traditionally defined.

The male "role" is not merely a list of traits, but takes meaning from its dynamic interplay with other roles. Men and women are not free-standing pieces of statuary, but are always interdefining. The dominant American tradition of manhood visualizes a lone figure against a vast horizon, on horseback in the Wild West version, a myth that denies the interactive dramas that make us who we are and sustain us in the selfhoods by which we know each other and ourselves.

Groups in power take roles that require the disempowered to assume supportive correlates, subordinate postures that acknowledge and bolster the position of their superiors. Yet the powerful are also required to sustain the existence that their place demands. "Why can't they live like white people?" a racist white woman once asked me about her white next-door neighbors, whose house and yard were unkempt. Men face similar imperatives to "be a man," behind which lies a gender bigotry enforced against women.

True intimacy rests on an interaction of selfhoods that is vital and healthy, with each party ingredient to the other's reality, yet mutually respectful and bearing equal dignity. But the ruling convention of gender defines "the masculine" and "the feminine" as opposites: growing boys are warned against "sissy stuff" and grown men are trapped in a permanent "flight from the feminine." This sharply dichotomous—indeed mutually hostile—relation of the "opposite sexes" becomes toxic when "the feminine" becomes the repository for the qualities men abhor in themselves. In maintaining traditional masculinity, the autoimmune attack on the self then becomes incorporated into relationships with women, and also with children and other men.

David Lisak notes that a hypermasculine man may respond to a crying baby with excessive anger because the wailing arouses buried torments that the man cannot endure to feel. As the baby comes to represent the man's disowned emotional vexations, it becomes an outward target of his manhood-sustaining inner rage. The violent loathing directed by zealots of code masculinity against gay men has also been found to originate in hysterical defensiveness, men desperately struggling to maintain faith in their own conventional manhood, so much so that Michael Kimmel has proposed that American manhood is fundamentally constituted by homophobia ("Masculinity").[6] Lisak indicates that sexual violence against women partakes of the same dynamic, arising when the woman's evident vulnerability triggers "resonant, unconscious emotions in the perpetrator." In attacking the woman, he attacks "these despised emblems of his vulnerability" (170-171).

This activity of the imagination, by which women are invested with meanings that originate in systemic male dilemmas, appears in a broad range of cultural forms.[7] Pornographic fascination is not provoked exclusively by images in movies and magazines: it is widely accepted as a romantic ideal, and it gives form to living relationships. Code manhood produces pornographic marriages, Terrence Real notes, in which the woman's compliance—whether voluntary or coerced—performs the man's need: "the essence of the pornographic vision of women is that they are so thoroughly 'in sync' with the male, that the things that give him pleasure just happen to drive her wild as well" (306). This promise gazes out from the covers of *Cosmopolitan, Redbook,* and *People*—inspiring men and women to dream of such fulfillment—even as its predictable abortive outcomes are emblazoned in the headlines of the *Star* and the *National Enquirer.*

Men who chronically batter and rape their wives further illustrate the syndrome in which men project the maladies of their own manhood into women. An abused wife is most acutely at risk when she seeks to terminate her relationship with the abuser, because this awakens the man's deep-lying dread of abandonment. But, as Donald Dutton asserts, "the men never frame the abandonment in terms of needing the woman and depending on her emotional support" (15). In order to preserve the illusion of their masculine self-sufficiency, such men project their self-loathing onto their mates. Dutton describes the resultant diatribe as "'playing the bitch tape,' which invariably contains the same four words: bitch, cunt, whore, slut" (16). The man's stereotyped but unconscious self-hatred sets this tape running in his head, and it then comes to consciousness as a torrent of abuse aimed at his spouse. Unaware of his dependency on her because he is ashamed of it, and unaware of hating himself for his neediness, the man projects on her the "bitch, cunt, whore, slut" that he feels himself to be. Like Captain Ahab in his demoniac hatred of the white whale, the abusive husband believes that his hateful inner womanhood is visibly embodied and made tangibly assailable in his wife.[8]

It has long seemed plausible that sexually abusive men were abused in childhood by women, especially when their assaults have a revengeful tone. An analogous line of argument holds that the appeal of pornography arises from the structures of a masculine identity that is formed in opposition to the feminine. Susan Griffin, Nancy Chodorow, and Dorothy Dinnerstein argue that males create an adult manhood over against their mothers, on whom they are wholly dependent—and with whom they are wholly identified—during infancy. "Mothers experience their sons as a male opposite," Chodorow writes, so that boys "are more likely [than girls] to have been pushed out of the pre-oedipal relationship and to have had to curtail their primary love and sense of empathic tie with their mother" (Pollack, "No Man" 41). Even when the task of creating an "opposite" identity is reasonably well completed, there remains an unconscious dread of women mingled with desire and hatred, a complex of impulses that threatens to undo the man's fragile manhood, which he seeks to consolidate by coercing women sexually or through the fantasies available in pornography. This thesis is borne out by the fact that pornography holds a special fascination for adolescent boys, in whom the processes of separating from the mother are particularly urgent (Gubar 63).

Yet the abuse that marks the early lives of sex offenders comes from fathers and other male figures more often than from women (Scully 67). Why would a man avenge himself for abuse at the hands of his father by raping women? Why would he be subject to pornographic enchantments? At least part of the answer lies in the definition of manhood that governs the rearing of boys. Parents acting on the belief that males and females are "opposite" sexes, allocating initiative and stoic self-possession to males while consigning nurture and vulnerability to females, instill a psychic organization in which growing boys cultivate a "girl" part of themselves, a counter-self from which disconcerting impulses continue to arise. It is hardly surprising that a man's early identification with his mother would appear inimical to the formation of his manhood, if manhood is understood *de novo* as anti-woman. Nor is it surprising that certain psychologists continue to warn—against the evidence—that women are unfit to rear sons without a "male model" in the household (see Real 144; Silverstein and Rashbaum).

Numerous scholars have traced the processes of socialization that instill the conventional pattern—at home, on the schoolground, and in boyhood sports. When these are accompanied by the infliction of physical or emotional cruelty, which sharpens the contrast between the anguished recipient of pain and the agent who produces it, a small boy learns to identify with the "male" figure who inflicts the punishment. "By impersonating the aggressor," Anna Freud wrote, "the child transforms himself from the person threatened into one who makes the threat" (Osherson 102). But this self-transformation entails a divided self; no amount of impersonation can cancel the actual vulnerability and terror, which live on through an opposing identity that the boy learns to disavow. Samuel Osherson declares that boys learn to become "men" through this "harsh milk of masculinity"; what he does not recognize is that such boys simultaneously (though tacitly) learn to be "women" (102–103).

Within the tough little boy is a hurt and frightened self—a self capable of tenderness and compassion. But the boy despises these traits, and considers them female, the opposite of himself. As he comes to maturity in the culture of code manhood, and increasingly makes war against his susceptibility to emotional distress, the young man acquires a maddening inner "bitch," which voices the distraction, humiliation, and panic that bedevil his masculinity, and he sees this "bitch" in actual women when they stir up his persistent inner pain.

The players in this covert intramale gender-drama sometimes become visible in a man's behavior. James Mitchell DeBardeleben II was a "sadistic" rapist, for whom the infliction of pain was erotically stimulating; instead of imagining that his victims enjoyed themselves, he made tape recordings of the reverse, accumulating a collection that he used to sustain his imaginative life during the intervals between crimes. DeBardeleben's fantasies of erotic cruelty become clear on these tapes. The shrieks and weeping of a victim are intercut by his commands, telling her to speak more clearly, to beg for more punishment, and to confess that she deserves it. It is a drama of two parts, that of the male master and that of the "SMB," his code for "sadomasochistic bitch." DeBardeleben also made tapes in which he plays both parts. A harsh cold voice assaults the SMB with degrading commands, and a groveling falsetto replies: "Yes, beat me, fuck me. I deserve it. I'm a no good bitch. I'm nothing but a little whore, a little bitch." Both voices are hysterically intense, the speaker fully invested in both, as DeBardeleben seeks relief in a scenario that splits him into two roles, the male torturer and the helpless woman he controls.[9]

A comparable drama is played out through the cross-dressing that occurs in about twenty percent of what are called autoerotic fatalities, when a man seeking sexual arousal subjects himself to mortal danger, typically near-asphyxiation, and accidentally kills himself. A man's body will be found hanging from the bar of a closet, wearing a bustier and lace stockings, or stretched on a bed in a negligee and panties, with a cord around his neck. Park Dietz quotes the handwritten notes of one such man who described his assumption of the "opposite" gender: "Now I slip the taffeta dress over my head and pull it down over my body. The base makeup starts to change my face into feminine softness, no sign of a beard. It takes ten minutes to put the lipstick on right. Now emerald rings, more jewelry. Now my blond wig transforms me into a woman completely" (Hazelwood, Dietz, and Burgess 35). The creator of this fatal charade in fact takes on both genders, that of the "woman" and that of the "man" who threatens her with death.

It is an appalling experience to sense a bond of shared manhood between oneself and perpetrators of extreme sexual violence. Ed Richards was an early member of the fellowship program that the FBI created to instruct local law enforcement officials in the profiling of sexual homicides. Richards became a specialist in crime scene analysis and consulted with police departments across Texas concerning such cases. "It's toxic work," he told me. "The emotional pressures accumulate and can bring you to the breaking point." He described the case of a nine-year-old girl who was tortured, raped, and murdered by three adults, one of whom was a feeble-minded young man who had been drawn into the crime by an older couple, a man and a woman. Richards mastered the complex particulars of the crime scene, which included several sites where the child received in sequence the numerous wounds discovered on her body.

Richards identified the killers, but he could not make a case, largely because the street-smart older couple successfully parried his investigation. Then he learned that the young man had been arrested in another matter, whereupon he set up an interview and obtained a full confession. "It took about three hours for him to describe the entire sequence of events, where the child was picked up, where she was taken . . ." Richards's many conjectures about the myriad details of evidence were now crystallized into a firm account. The feeble-minded young killer was drained with exhaustion when the ordeal ended and sat for a moment in silence. Then getting out of his chair he climbed into Richards's lap, put his arms around his neck, and rested his head against the investigator's shoulder like a child seeking comfort. "That did it for me," Richards said. "It took a lot of therapy to get me back to normal. I realized I'd done as much of these investigations as I could stand." Richards found his way into another line of police work soon thereafter.

As an FBI-trained specialist in the investigation of sexual homicide, Richards had the strongest social sanction for his involvement in rape-murders, yet this was not sufficient to counteract the emotional distress that came to a head as the young criminal sought solace from him. A man can steel himself against the horror of crime scene after crime scene, and form plausible interpretations of their ghastly details, by relying upon ingrained manly traits of self-possession under pressure. But how is he to manage an appeal for comfort from a doomed young creature whom he himself has tracked down? How can he accept the embrace of the sex-killer without sensing his own complicity, the occult communion of the hunter with his quarry, established through their shared stake in the scene of the crime and culminating at its final elucidation? How can he reject that embrace without denying his own humanity, his pity for the wretchedness underlying the insane cruelty of the young man's crime?

Most of all, how can he give comfort at this moment without becoming aware of his own need for comfort, his own exhaustion under the long burden of playing the manly part? How can he serve as a caregiver here, how adopt a maternal and nurturant stance just here, as the long tension of his investigation is finally ended and the prize of a full confession has been secured and recorded on tape, without being taken out to sea by the running tide of his own pain and long-suspended need?

Richards deserves admiration for breaking down. Instead of stifling his capacity for tenderness and compassion—or being deafened by a "bitch tape"—he gave way to the "womanly" impulses that the exercise of his strenuous and heroic manhood had brought to the surface. He did not take refuge in a paroxysm of loathing toward the criminal, or in obscene humor, or in psychic deadening. Still, he was ill served by the conventions of gender that delayed his encounter with his own distress and produced a disabling crisis that for a time monopolized all his working energy. Self-possession in the face of disorienting pain is incontestably a desirable trait, desirable for women as well as for men. It is also desirable for men to be capable of feeling their own vulnerability and helplessness, of giving way for a spell to anguish and dismay, and of reaching out for help.

Carl Jung believed that men possess a "feminine" side and can achieve psychic wholeness only through acknowledging and living out the contrasexual identity within them. Jung's work inaugurated a tradition of therapy that aims toward achieving a "conjunction" of the masculine and feminine "opposites."[10] The contemporary Jungian Roger Horrocks argues accordingly that misogyny denotes a failure of healthy self-realization: "the hatred of women connects with a hatred of the inner feminine in men—both must be crushed for men to be 'men'" (90).

Jung viewed "the masculine" and "the feminine" as fixed and universal psychic realities, not as conceptions subject to the political and economic conditions of the societies in which they are generated. He thus enlarged upon definitions of manhood and womanhood that were produced—as we shall see—during the late eighteenth century, in a Euro-American society where men virtually monopolized the institutions that seek and authenticate knowledge.

Exclusive power to define "the feminine" is not so obvious as more tangible forms of male domination, since it belongs to the domain of imagination; yet it is nonetheless injurious. Garry Wills has argued that John Wayne's popularity rests on his projecting a compelling pattern of manly virtue, and that indispensable to this pattern is the sexualized coercion of women. "All you gotta have in a John Wayne movie," remarked Wayne's favorite writer, Jimmy Grant, "is a hoity-toity dame with big tits that Duke can throw over his knees and spank" (Wills, *Wayne's America* 278) The Jungian feminine—like conventional femininity—does not arise from the experience of women but is a male experience that men have through women.

The "feminine" is like music in a man's mind, distinctively man-music; but he cannot grasp it, cannot hum it to himself without losing track of it. If he is to enjoy it, women have to sing it for him, and his pleasure includes the satisfaction of thinking it is their music not his. The "masculine" perhaps plays a comparable role in women's lives, voicing capacities that women have been socialized to deny in themselves. The mysterious processes by which personhoods are woven together through mutual projections—men and women finding their deepest selves in one another—are not always pernicious. None of us is equal to his or her own experience; none of us exists in isolation. The passionate absorption of lovers in each other's souls, like the rich interplay that informs the memories and immediate experience of persons in long-term relationships, shows that autonomy itself is a product of the intercourse that sustains us.

Thus we return to Whitman's paradox, to acknowledge its genuinely democratic potential. The invocation of egalitarian principle has not only served as a cover for male supremacy, but has emboldened women to claim substantive rights equal to those of men, and has inspired men to cooperate in building more equitable institutions. M. Jacqui Alexander and Chandra Mohanty frame the paradox this way: they define Democracy (capital "D") as a rhetorical tradition that disguises sexism, racism, and Western imperialism, in contrast to democracy (lowercase d) that sponsors the creation of communities "premised on ideas of autonomy and self-determination, in other words democratic practice" (xxxvii). The folkways that offer justifications for sexual violence against women rest on deep-running American traditions, but the opposition to those folkways is also grounded in the American creed and spells out its central truths.

Long before the feminist debates of our own time, it was understood that equal rights for women did not require women to become like men.[11] Margaret Fuller asserted the core principle when she declared that freedom entails women's discovering their own womanhoods, individually and collectively, freed from the conventions of gender that were produced to serve male interests. Fuller asserted that men can neither embody an ideal for women nor define one, because men believe that "Woman was made *for Man.*" A fit understanding of womanhood will be constructed by women, Fuller declared. What must be enforced is women's right to construct it. "We would have every arbitrary barrier thrown down" so that a woman is enabled "as a nature to grow, as an intellect to discern, as a soul to live freely and unimpeded, to unfold such powers as were given her" (247–248).

Fuller's program for women, and the courage she showed in proposing it, might serve today as an inspiration for men. The code manhood that produces sexual violence against women ensnares men who lead lives of quiet desperation, alienated from the truth of their experience. The social and economic rewards of performing the male masquerade are substantial, but even for the successful they come at a grievous psychic cost. The cost for women is obscene and will remain so as long as men retain the power to impose conceptions of the "feminine" that perpetuate the masquerade at the expense of women. Yet men too have a stake in undoing this injustice, so as to fashion more truthful self-understandings and come to know women on terms that presuppose their equality, not their subservience.

3

Becoming a Natural Man

THE YOUNG MEN WERE shoved into the showers and forced to drink emetics while buckets of diluted shit were thrown on them. Soon all were vomiting, and they were made to grovel in the filth; then they were hogtied and carried downstairs to a dark basement. This is a fraternity initiation, as described by Peggy Reeves Sanday in *Fraternity Gang Rape*. "The pledges were forced into caskets, and the lids were closed . . . Screams and moans could be heard from within the caskets, as well as sounds of pounding as the pledges thrashed around inside. These noises were quickly drowned out by brothers loudly chanting, 'Die pussies die, die pussies die'" (161).

Fraternity gang rapes are a version of the same ritual, Sanday demonstrates; they confirm a misogynist manhood that identifies women with excrement and death. Yet the male solidarity produced by initiation is also founded on the abuse of males by males. Such brutality is not found in all fraternity initiations—nor are all fraternities guilty of gang rape—but the ritual Sanday describes conforms to a familiar pattern, which was established in fraternal organizations during the late nine-teenth century. Initiates pass through a period of stress that is managed by full-fledged members, and after their ordeal they accept the brotherly friendship of the men who tormented them. As Mark Carnes has shown, such ceremonies are a gendered version of death and resurrection, where the initiates die to a feminine self—in this instance a "pussy" self—and rise fit to join the world of adult males (116–127). But the ordeal that counts as "death" is inflicted on men by men.

Inductees are execrated as "pussies" as they enter military life, and cognate rituals mark the threshold of participation in con-tact sports—especially football—that are considered analogous to warfare. The threat of death is intrinsic to such initiations, and it often happens that recruits, ballplayers, and fraternity initiates are killed in the course of seeking the manhood that the ritual is meant to instill. Gang rapes and other forms of sex-ual abuse are committed with notable frequency by soldiers, athletes, and fraternity men.

These subcultures carry forward an American tradition of sexually abusive manhood. Alternative manhoods, which also have historical ancestors, are alive in contemporary society, but the validity of such alternatives is not acknowledged by the cer-emonies that induct young men into warrior cults.[1] On the con-trary, such initiations insist that the warrior model is identical to manhood itself and promise that the neophytes will become "real men." This fraudulent claim enjoys widespread authority in American life: successful soldiers are thought to possess bedrock male competence, fitting them for supreme responsibilities. George Washington, Andrew Jackson, Ulysses Grant, Theodore Roosevelt, and Dwight Eisenhower were popular presidents; Gerald Ford and Jack Kemp advertised their exploits as football players; and Ronald Reagan managed to derive prestige from having played a broken-field runner in the movies.

This American tradition has antecedents in prehistory, so ancient that tracing them in detail is not feasible. Barbara Ehrenreich argues plausibly that a sacred aura came to surround warrior heroism when wolves, hyenas, and the great cats routinely preyed on human beings. Serving as food for animals awakened primordial terror, Ehrenreich proposes, whose traces are visible in religious traditions that envision the gods as carnivores requiring blood sacrifice. The prowess of early hunters was invested with religious portent because it aided in counteracting that terror; and the skills required for hunting predators gained additional prestige when they were sophisticated for use against other human beings. Intergroup raiding may have been practiced by our primate forebears; it is practiced today by chimps and gorillas. But early human societies developed warrior elites that were formalized in distinctively human ways. As they brought their communities to the top of the food chain, the warrior class transformed hunting and gathering bands into tribes capable of plundering other tribes and of excluding rivals from desirable territories.

In *The Human Condition,* William McNeill describes the formation of these warrior elites, whose fighting skills allowed them to exploit the labor of subject peoples through plunder and taxation. Yet despite their exemption from productive toil, the warriors were trapped in the world they made. Since deadly force prevails against every countering measure except deadly force, they were chronically at war with their counterparts in neighboring societies (5–8). Arms-race logic forced ancient peoples down the road toward mutual destruction before any records were kept; and the basic system, once established, was destined to persist with myriad variations in city states, kingdoms, maritime empires, and modern nations. David Gilmore's comparative study of manhoods in twentieth-century societies indicates that the survival value of this "pressured" form of manhood varies with the demands of the environment, including the presence or absence of potentially hostile neighbors (*Manhood* 220). Women have a significant political voice in hunter/gatherer societies surviving today, since their economic contribution is as critical as that of men to collective welfare. But in the warrior structure, and its historical descendants, economic production is held hostage to military power, and women take part in governance through connections with men.

The disparagement of women became a feature of warrior manhood at an early time. In *The History of Warfare* John Keegan discusses cultural differences among traditions of warfare, and historical changes that have altered these cultures in the West. Yet he finds a warrior ethos common to such disparate settings. Since the effectiveness of a fighting unit depends on coordinated action, and since fleeing men are readily cut down, panic is suicidal. Killing human beings inspires revulsion in those who do it, also, and this revulsion must be conquered in the making of a warrior. Membership in early warrior elites entailed a subjective discipline, in which panic and squeamishness were scorned as womanish. Ehrenreich traces the long tradition in which "men who failed as warriors have been reviled as 'women'" (126). Fraternity rituals—like their counterparts in the military and sports—seek to instill warrior virtue on these terms; their death-and-rebirth rituals exorcise the "pussy"; they kill off the qualities that make an initiate the contemptible opposite of a man.

We have yet to understand, however, why such rituals take place in college fraternities. Very few brothers will face combat, even if they serve in the military. For most, finding advancement in large bureaucratic organizations will tell the difference between success and failure. Even if they work in small-scale settings, young men will find that containing hostility is critical to forming productive business and professional relationships, which increasingly include relationships with women. Few middle-class men earn an income—as sole wage earners—sufficient to maintain and perpetuate a family's middle-class status, an economic weakness that seems likely to endure. Male college graduates will continue to occupy dual-career households in which the woman is a breadwinner. Do men prepare for this future by execrating themselves and one another as "pussies"?

Contemporary young American men inherit a tradition that has taken the warrior code from warrior life and made it a "natural" imperative, a genetically programmed character that men must fulfill if they are to attain true manhood. At first glance this seems absurd: no human being acts in a way forbidden by his or her genetic constitution. But this version of masculinity succeeds nonetheless in proposing the inevitable as obligatory. The fusion of "natural manhood" with warrior manhood took place in our early national period, and while the tradition has passed through significant changes in the intervening two centuries, it is very much alive today.

Modern college fraternities act out a theory of "nature" that was used to champion democracy in the battle against bloodline aristocracy in the eighteenth century. Before the democratic era, the societies of Western Europe embraced the theory that men are created unequal, some ordained by God to rule, others to live in subjection. Against the new standard of manhood equality, hereditary entitlements were judged despotic, the rule of illegitimate brute force. But democratic theory was itself twisted to secure the continued political domination of women by men. "Natural manhood" was taken to mean that men are equally entitled to rule over women, who fulfill their "natural" womanhood in subservience. Warrior manhood, now visualized as a quality all men equally possess, perpetuated despotic power into the democratic era. Contemporary gang rapes dramatize the social dynamics of the resultant system, in which a despotic warrior manhood is secured through the degradation of women.

Eighteenth-century advocates of democratic theory—John Locke and Jean Jacques Rousseau—envisioned a primordial "state of nature," in which individual men led solitary lives in keeping with the dictates of nature and nature's God. Human society came next, formed when such individuals agreed to a "social contract," each giving up the liberty of his independent existence so as to secure the advantages of life in a civil community. As freely contracting equal partners, "natural men" created the social bond itself, from which it follows that governments derive legitimacy from the consent of the governed.

But social contract theory is patently false. What we know about our primate cousins, and about early human history, demonstrates that we are *de novo* social animals: individual existence is unthinkable apart from the society into which we are born. Social contract theory retroactively imposes an ideology of consent upon circumstances that are coercive, and meets protest with the claim that coercion had been agreed to.

Fraternity ritual dramatizes this paradoxical situation. All of the pledges have agreed to go through the initiation, and in theory they could opt out. But they have agreed to coercion. Although participation is voluntary, they have contracted to accept involuntary experiences, to spasms of defecation and vomiting, to runaway panic. The critical moment in such rituals arrives when uncontrollable aversion is awakened and the pledge struggles desperately to resist the torments to which he has consented. A margin of choice remains, but the ritual attains its meaning when that margin is felt to disappear.

Such rituals are appealing because a college man is living through a time of life in which the ambiguities of consent provoke severe anxieties. The ideology of democratic individualism tells him he is moving toward what we call a "career," a life course that he himself will direct, freely choosing a major and a mate in keeping with his plans. His eventual success depends, so the theory tells him, on the hard work and self-discipline he commits to pursuing his goals. But college men also feel the power of conditions they cannot control.

White males enjoy advantages of race denied to others, and all males enjoy advantages of gender. Among those favored by race and gender, the differences are substantial. Athletic and intellectual talent opens doors for some that remain closed to others; neurotic difficulties disrupt the lives of some, while others are sustained by a legacy of psychic health; some count on career opportunities that follow from social privilege, while others have no useful contacts except those they hope to find in the fraternity. In order to maintain faith in themselves as self-directing agents, young men must discount these facts, giving consent where they know themselves to be helpless.

Sanday rightly claims that fraternity initiations assert male privilege at the expense of women. But the male experience of privilege is far from monolithic; the initiation reinforces male solidarity not only against women but against fierce tacit conflicts that set the men against one another and themselves. Exorcising the "pussy" banishes the accumulated resentments and anxieties that threaten to undermine masculine self-possession. The ritual exists in order to claim, against the evidence, that the men are "brothers." The denigration of women is a means to that end.

This becomes starkly clear in the accompanying tradition of gang rape, which plays out the ambiguities of consent with a difference. The male initiate agrees beforehand to coercion; but consent is imputed to the rape victim after she is coerced. When the rapists defend themselves, they typically focus on the moment when, as they see it, the victim signed the contract, when it became clear she was "asking for it." A signing ceremony goes this way: it is late at night, after a party with much drinking; the woman makes what is construed as a signal of willingness—passionately kisses one of the brothers, dances wildly to rock and roll, goes upstairs to her date's bedroom.

The process is known as "working a yes out," Sanday explains, which means that the men succeed in eliciting a gesture that cancels the right of future refusal. Once she is "compromised," it matters little that the woman is disoriented with fatigue and alcohol or goes upstairs with her date because she is frightened by the crowd of brothers. If she has sex with her date, the waiting brothers are at liberty to proceed, since any subsequent resistance will be subsumed under the consent she is imagined to have given already.

The laws defining rape generally conspire with this vicious scenario; they avoid the issue of consent and focus exclusively on the use of force, leaving unrecognized the reality of coerced—or fraudulently obtained—consent (Schulhofer 99–103, 254–273). The social agreement sustaining this failure of the law likewise maintains that the gang-raped woman must surely have known what was going on—and have given her consent—during the process that carried her into the trap. In *A Woman Scorned*, Sanday examines a case in which a young woman was systematically intimidated, pressed to consume vodka until she was virtually unconscious, subjected to multiple vaginal and oral penetrations, and held responsible by the courts. Like the fraternity initiate, the rape victim becomes a "pussy"—but not temporarily. Instead of leading to acceptance as a "brother," the ritual makes her an embodiment of what the brothers despise in themselves.

As Sanday notes, this concoction of fantasy and deceit feels "natural" to the men involved (*Fraternity* 87–89). A trancelike state descends in which they seem to obey imperatives lying deep in their constitution, beneath conscious awareness. "It was weird," one of them said, as he described the tacit collusion through which the group had carried out a multiple rape. "I knew what was going on without ever being told. I think everyone knew" (69). The decorum of civilized life, with its noxious laws and prohibitions, is felt to dissolve, giving way to liberated spontaneity, in which the rapists feel that their own aggression, and the woman's imagined consent, enact a "state of nature" sexuality. "Natural manhood" here seems to meet "natural womanhood" in defiance of social pieties.

The logic of this atrocity was articulated by Jean Jacques Rousseau in the eighteenth century, but Rousseau did not view it as an atrocity. On the contrary, he justified the self-excusing rigmarole put forward by rapists on the basis of natural law. Arguing that the social relations of men and women should conform to the purposes for which nature fitted them, Rousseau declared that nature ordains sexual assault.

"Woman is made to please and to be subjugated," he asserted; she yields to a man's advances "merely because he is strong" (359). Rousseau concedes that this is "not the law of love" but "that of nature, prior to love itself" (358). He explains that a woman is always asking for it, since this follows from her womanly being. A natural sexual encounter begins when her "charms" stir the man to use force, and goes forward as her struggle aids in arousing him. The woman "repulses him and always defends herself" whether she "shares man's desires or not": otherwise the encounter would be spoiled. If she wants to have sex, there's no need for him to take her by force, which is the only way he can fulfill his nature. "What is sweetest for man in his victory," Rousseau comments, "is the doubt whether it is weakness which yields to strength or the will which surrenders. And the woman's usual ruse is always to leave this doubt between her and him" (360).

Modern American rapists want to believe that the victim has consented when she has not, while Rousseau's natural man wants to believe that the woman has not consented when she has. These two views are not in contradiction; they are alternative expressions of the same reality, in which sexual assault is seen to proceed from the intrinsic nature of manhood and womanhood. Like his twentieth-century descendants, Rousseau is eager to separate this schema of male attack and unavailing female defense from what he calls "real rape," in which the woman seeks to defend herself "at the expense of the aggressor's life" (359). "Real rape" does not happen when a woman is rendered incapable of consent, or when consent is made to justify subsequent coercion, but only when she mounts a life-and-death battle to resist. In *Unwanted Sex,* Stephen Schulhofer abundantly documents the contention that this logic governs the legal definition of rape in contemporary America. Unless a woman bears the marks of a battle in deadly earnest, it will be assumed that she invited the attack. Her claim of rape, as Rousseau foretold, will "attract the laughter of mockers" (360).

The manhood that Rousseau proclaimed "natural" was a social product, a style of masculinity shaped by the historical circumstances in which it arose and the ideological struggles in which it was useful. The ancient warrior code, itself having arisen and evolved under shifting historical conditions, was absorbed into an ideal of despotic natural manhood in the era of democratic revolution. In America warrior manhood was democratized as a dictate of nature, to which all men should equally conform, and this process assigned to women a distinctive set of supporting roles, including the role of blameworthy victim assigned to targets of gang rape. To understand the contemporary force of these perverse conceptions, we must examine the historical developments that established the despotic warrior ideal as a standard of manly worth for American men.

———

Absolutist monarchs sought to limit the scope of European wars during the century and a half that elapsed between the Thirty Years War and the French Revolution. Dependent on economies increasingly controlled by a rising capitalist class, these rulers were reluctant to place military power in the hands of the populace at large, lest the basis of their monarchical supremacy be further eroded. Military forces were officered by nobility, and the rank and file was drawn from a rabble of drunks, beggars, and petty criminals. Regular soldiers served in a military equivalent of prison, where they were drilled incessantly in the tedious complexities of maintaining the formations that directed musket fire. Native armies were hard to recruit and expensive to maintain, and were typically complemented by equally expensive mercenary units, so that monarchs had good reason to be frugal in deploying and engaging them. Battles during this period had the look of massive, elaborate minuets— at least by comparison with the wholesale slaughter that was soon to come—and these battles were carried out by specialists who lived a life distinct from civil society and separated from it.

The "shot heard round the world" in 1775 in Concord, Massachusetts, ushered in not only a new era of political democracy but a new era of soldiering as well. The colonial militias that fought for independence from Britain were inspired by the impulse to gain full possession of the civil community, not to lead a professional soldier's life outside it. The drive toward democratic citizenship transformed European nations; it abolished the gulf between the army and society and made soldiering the shared destiny of men. John Keegan sums up the change: "In the span of twenty years a European society in which only those men existing at the economic margin risked incorporation into the ranks, had become militarized from top to bottom, and . . . the soldier's life, hitherto known only to a willing or more usually unwilling minority, had become the common experience" (*History* 349).

The French National Convention called for a *levée en masse* in August 1793, and by the beginning of the following year had an army of unprecedented size, numbering 1,169,000 men (ibid. 233). The "rights of man" thus came to mean the rights of men at arms, so that the new political freedom brought with it new terrors. "The prerevolutionary regular soldiers had been scarce and expensive," Gwynne Dyer remarks, but "the lives of conscripts were plentiful and cheap. The disdain for casualties grew even greater once Napoleon had seized control of France in 1799. 'You cannot stop me,' he boasted to Count Metternich, the Austrian diplomat; 'I spend thirty thousand men a month'" (69).

The army that gained independence for the American colonies under George Washington was not an army of mass conscription; it followed the traditional pattern of gentleman leaders, low-life regulars, and mercenary hirelings. But patriotic volunteers also played a role, and when the war was over a controversy erupted concerning officers' pensions that indicated how deeply democratic ideals were now intertwined with warrior ideals. Officers demanded five-year pensions that would provide a bridge to the life of gentry privilege, perpetuating the upper-class status they had presumably confirmed by commanding their inferiors in battle. This proposal met fierce opposition by men who had served as soldier-citizens in the rank and file, and it was soon abandoned. Thomas Jefferson denounced such measures as innately "hostile to 'the natural equality of man' and conducive to 'habits of subordination' and the subversion of liberty" (Royster, *Revolutionary* 354).

The "natural equality of man" came to mean that the sovereignty earlier reserved to the monarch, and diffusely present in the nobility, is now inherent to every male citizen, taking the form of inalienable rights. A "natural man" is entitled to back his decisions by force, to rebel against the current government, or to place his personal capacity for violence at its disposal. Ralph Waldo Emerson summed up the new order as one in which "man will treat with man as a sovereign state with a sovereign state" (72). The male body—conceived as the body of a warrior—served as natural evidence of this sovereignty. It is no accident that zealots of code manhood in our own time insist—against the ruling tradition of constitutional interpretation—that the right to bear arms is an individual right.

In *National Manhood*, Dana Nelson demonstrates that this brand of masculinity was not deemed inherent to all men; despite invocations of God-given equality, this convention mobilized powerful anti-democratic prejudices. Black men and Native American men were excluded from the hegemonic version, despite their potentially more plausible claim to actual warrior proficiencies. On the contrary, like women, nonwhite men were incorporated into the new moral economy as holders of economic value that white males could properly seize and control, and eventually as subjects for scientific experimentation that sought to measure exactly the "natural" deficiencies that disqualified them from full equality. A fraternal mystique of individual self-sovereignty was merged into the national myth, but membership was limited to white men, especially those possessing the means of economic self-advancement.[2]

This notion of warrior manhood became a dominant ideal in America, moreover, during a period in which very few citizens served in the military. Between the Revolution and the Civil War, only the War of 1812 and the Mexican War prompted calls for soldiers. American life was militarized not because of large-scale battlefield service but because civilian life in the new nation was experienced as combat.

Capitalism in America swiftly surmounted the folkways of inherited privilege and mutual responsibility that had prevailed in colonial times. In *The Market Revolution,* Charles Sellers describes the "almost unlimited opportunities for profit" that became available to new enterprises in commercial production and overseas shipping, which increased American exports fivefold between 1790 and 1807 and sponsored an explosive growth of wealth and population in Philadelphia, New York, Boston, and Baltimore (22–23). The new nation quickly became a testing ground for the ideals of Adam Smith, with his vision of the market economy as an interplay of self-interested and self-governing centers of initiative. As face-to-face communities of status and obligation were swept aside by urbanization and westward expansion, entrepreneurs pursued their ambitions among fierce competitors and quickly became acclimated to persistent and uncertain conflict.

Men who worked with their hands were also newly conceived as "individuals." Having "acquired what were in effect property rights over themselves," Robert Wiebe explains, "they were disentangled from family and status networks" (13). Yet with only their time and skills to market, laborers were compelled to adopt the ideal of individual opportunity on terms that increased their vulnerability. The European artisan tradition prevailing in the colonies had awarded skilled workers the right to a decent living because they provided goods and services that were necessary to community well-being. Now stripped of the protections that followed from this social agreement, working men found their livelihoods becoming considerably more precarious, especially in the booming urban centers (Sellers 23–24). Men who began life as artisans sometimes achieved economic success, but those who fell victim to economic misfortune were held personally answerable. "This is a country of *self-made men*," declared an ideologue of the new order; "the idle, lazy, poor man gets little pity in his poverty" (ibid. 238).

Small merchants, like men in the professional classes, might attain a degree of affluence, at times a considerable degree. But few could secure the future for their offspring; nearly all young men were required to pass through a period of self-reliant upward striving. Despite the advantages enjoyed by middle-class males in contrast with the children of laborers, they nonetheless faced a struggle with no guarantee of success, in which unremitting competitive struggle was required.

Sellers observes that this era witnessed a dramatic widening of the gap between wealth and poverty, belying the middle-class myth of equal opportunity. "Nor were the wealthy self-made," he continues, "overwhelmingly they were sons of rich and/or eminent families" (238). Ordinary men could reasonably hope to secure a decent competence, not great wealth, through self-directed efforts, even as they were haunted by the prospect of "ruin," economic failure all the more wretched because shameful.

Still, the first decades of national independence placed considerable opportunities before white men, and by the end of the eighteenth century there had developed a society of middling fortunes based on the self-directed work of farmers and local entrepreneurs. As Sellers explains, this majority culture of relative white-male equality was supplanted once roads and canals (and eventually railways) permitted large-scale capitalist enterprises to reach national markets and concentrated economic and political power in a small ownership class while consigning most working men to the ranks of industrial labor. Sellers concludes that the claim to equal rights, despite its usefulness to exponents of capitalist domination, also provided strategies by which its victims could defend themselves: "Contrary to liberal mythology, democracy was born in tension with capitalism, and not as its natural and legitimizing political expression" (32). There remains this conflict within the American tradition of democratic equality: it is routinely invoked to rationalize the domination of privileged men over others (and all men over women); at the same time it persists as a standard by which the oppressed demand liberation.[3]

Michael Kimmel and Anthony Rotundo sum up the harsh contrasts and internal contradictions presented by this "era of the self-made man" (Kimmel, *Manhood* chs. 2–3; Rotundo 18–25). It offered exhilarating opportunities for men who had known the frustration of being trapped economically beneath bloodline aristocracies in Europe or landed gentry in colonial America; yet the new order mercilessly exploited blacks, Native Americans, recent immigrants, and women. And the unceasing scramble for wealth imposed a psychic cost on the relatively fortunate. Alexis de Tocqueville commented on the "strange melancholy which often haunts the inhabitants of democratic countries in the midst of their abundance." He traced it to the "universal competition" that clogs the pathway to individual success with a "dense throng" of equally ardent careerists (138–139). Nathaniel Hawthorne called it the "agony of the universal struggle to wrest the means of existence from a host of greedy competitors" (*Notebooks* 332).

In the political realm as well, democratic equality implied that the path to power was open to every man. "In a country where offices are created solely for the benefit of the people," declared President Andrew Jackson, "no one man has any more intrinsic right to official station than another" (Wood 304). In *The Radicalism of the American Revolution*, Gordon Wood describes the political competition of newly liberated equal individuals as it supplanted elaborate hierarchies of privilege and dependency. It was fatal, in the new politics, to be identified as an "aristocrat," and men of gentry status sought office by adopting the manner of the common man. "They are absolutely on the same footing as the rest of the citizens," said Tocqueville. "They are dressed the same . . . are accessible at every moment, and shake everybody by the hand" (ibid. 304).

Janet Appleby explains that handshaking became the preferred form of masculine salutation because it expressed "parity and warmth" (134). At presidential receptions George Washington greeted citizens with a formal bow from the dais; but Thomas Jefferson mingled with them, shaking hands, and often opened the door himself when his guests showed up at the White House (134). Such affability obscured chronic anxiety; it was required by the uncertainties of mobilizing electorates in the new era of mass politics, when party loyalty became a paramount virtue and the "spoils system" decreed that current officeholders might well be ousted following the next election. Like the capitalist economy, democratic politics favored privilege and created it—but only temporarily. The new baseline reality was relentless individual competition.

David Leverenz traces the cultural transformation though which this "entrepreneurial" manhood asserted its dominance over the "patrician" and "artisan" manhoods of the colonial era (72-107). George Washington remained a model of patrician dignity, but the American literature of the early nineteenth century increasingly depicts men of gentry status—with their powdered wigs—as ridiculous fops. The new political order provided opportunities for resistance to the anti-democratic features of the rising capitalist economy, but it also offered mechanisms by which the beneficiaries of that economy could secure their interests. At midcentury Walt Whitman adopted the stance of the honest artisan—the carpenter, the blacksmith, the shoemaker—as an icon of democratic independence, even as industrial capitalism increasingly consigned such craftsmen to proletarian labor.

The turbulent new society broke through the social controls earlier enforced by traditional hierarchies of authority and deference. "Everything seemed to be coming apart," Gordon Wood observes; "social authority and the patronage power of the magistrates and gentry were no longer able to keep the peace" (306–307). The face-to-face networks of small-town life disintegrated in the anonymous urban spaces where "new men" sought to make their way. The dramatically increased consumption of alcohol offered solace against the new stresses but did nothing to diminish them, and increasing personal violence came to include fistfights in state legislatures and on the floor of Congress. Frequent urban riots prompted a demand for the creation of professional police forces. "A new competitiveness was abroad," Wood remarks, which emboldened ordinary men to pursue unprecedented dreams of personal achievement; yet at times these men "seemed almost at war with one another" (307).

A new vogue of dueling indicates clearly how the practices of traditional warrior class were absorbed into the competitive ethos. The *code duello,* as Appleby explains, had taken form among men of leisure in European societies and was indulged in mostly by army officers who fought over gambling debts and women. But in the United States dueling became endemic to partisan politics, killing more than a hundred men (and wounding many more) in the first two decades of the nineteenth century. Political controversies often involved personal affronts, which prompted claims of insulted honor, and the resultant challenges were hard to refuse for any man who valued his reputation (30, 41–45). Before he was killed by Aaron Burr, Alexander Hamilton survived ten challenges and lost his son Philip to a supporter of Thomas Jefferson. Andrew Jackson, Stephen Decatur, Michael Taney, and John Randolph fought duels, as did a multitude of less famous political leaders, and newspaper editors were often caught up in the mayhem. Persistent efforts to restrain dueling were unavailing until the late 1830s, blocked by those who viewed "the right to protect one's reputation as one of those 'certain natural rights inalienable' above the law" (43). Personal violence was ingredient, that is, to the natural manhood that every male citizen was imagined to embody.

The economic and political arrangements democratizing warrior manhood were symbolized, but also intensified, by the conquest of the frontier. Warfare with the native inhabitants of western lands was virtually continuous in the early national period, and it became an emblem for the battle that frontier settlers waged with the hardships of isolated living, unpredictable weather, and the effort to grow crops or raise cattle in unfamiliar surroundings. The literature depicting this struggle was not addressed to the persons who undertook it; they did not have time for reading and could hardly be reached by booksellers. Books about trapping, hunting, and Indian-fighting out west were written for middle-class urban Americans and portrayed the trials of frontiersmen as a screen on which the readers' own individualist strivings were projected.

James Fenimore Cooper's Leather-Stocking Tales played out the romance of this struggle, as did the legendary feats of actual men—like Davy Crockett, Sam Houston, and Andrew Jackson—who became celebrities in the East. In *Regeneration through Violence*, Richard Slotkin traces the mythology that came to surround Daniel Boone in the early nineteenth century, making him a national hero because of solitary wilderness exploits in which personal violence carries him through crisis after crisis (268–312). In *Studies in Classic American Literature*, D. H. Lawrence singled out Cooper's Leather-Stocking as an embodiment of "the essential American soul," because he is "hard, isolate, stoic and a killer" (73).

A prophetic minority of women invoked democratic principle to mount a challenge against the male privilege that the new culture of warrior manhood sought to perpetuate. The struggle of women to obtain economic and political equality was strong enough to require a defensive response from men and constituted a major feature in the new landscape of gender.

As the United States Constitution was being drafted, Abigail Adams wrote her famous letter to her husband, John, requesting that he enlarge the civil powers of women since they should not be compelled to obey a government in which they had no representation. Mary Wollstonecraft's *Vindication of the Rights of Women*, published fourteen years later, found a ready audience in America among women who had realized that the traditional subordination of women violated their inherent rights. In 1793 Priscilla Mason presented a valedictory address at the Young Ladies Academy of Philadelphia in which she advanced the classic case against male despotism: "Being the stronger party . . . [men] seized the sceptre and the sword; with these they gave laws to society . . . They doomed the [female] sex to servile or frivolous employments, on purpose to degrade their minds

. . . The Church, the Bar, and the Senate are shut against us. Who shut them? *Man,* despotic man, first made us incapable of the duty, and then forbid us the exercise" (Lerner 214).

The doctrine of "natural" genders was carefully elaborated to defend male privilege from this challenge. Males and females are ordained by nature to fundamentally unlike characters, the ideologues insisted. They cannot be measured by the same standard, and their complementary "opposite" virtues must be pursued along completely distinct pathways. The political and economic rights of men in a democracy were denied to women on the ground that exercising those rights would violate their womanly nature. Rousseau's "natural" woman, coquettishly inviting male assault, was not promoted as a positive ideal for women in antebellum American culture, but it took form as a powerful anti-type. The new model of womanhood was a two-fold affair, the angel/whore dichotomy, and both sides of the dichotomy were concocted to serve male interests and to resist women's efforts to attain democratic rights.

The new gender system perpetuated subordination by requiring that "true womanhood" must be lived out in "woman's sphere," namely the middle-class home. The domestic ideal, promoted as the natural expression of womanly gentleness and nurture, envisioned the home as a sanctuary where the man enjoyed an intimate and confiding life that was denied him in his contention with other men. The virtues of compassion and nurturant tenderness allocated to women are real virtues, which men systematically repressed in conforming to the demands of worldly warfare. Commenting in 1997 on the pathologies that continue to flow from this tradition of manhood, David Lisak confirms that being "disconnected" from one's emotional vulnerabilities and those of others "renders one a formidable soldier in any theatre of combat" (161). The culture of the early nineteenth century recognized the psychic cost and defined the home as a place of refuge. Women were assigned responsibility for providing intimate solace to men whose emotional capacities were handicapped.

Women who entered the public order seeking democratic rights were condemned for having stepped outside their natural sphere. Early feminists like Wollstonecraft and the Grimké sisters were execrated as gender-monsters, freaks of nature with "masculine minds" and "masculine manners." The president of Yale College, Timothy Dwight, condemned Wollstonecraft not only as a "hoyden" and a "non-descript"—both terms suggesting a sexually anomalous nature—but also as a "strumpet" (Kerber 279-283).

Women who took no part in feminist activism also fell victim to the angel/whore dichotomy. Domestic angels were conceived as divinely pure, yet as drastically contaminated if they strayed from the path of virtue, whereupon they become suitable targets for sexual abuse by men. Helen Benedict, in *Virgin or Vamp*, discusses the twentieth-century persistence of this dichotomy in the media representation of sexual crimes. The "slut" or "pussy" who undergoes fraternity gang rape is likewise a victim of the gender injustice we have inherited from the early nineteenth century, when the whore/angel dichotomy became conventional.

The "domestic angel" solaced male needs that arose in the competitive strife beyond the sacrosanct home; the "whore" served needs that arose because worldly warfare in fact penetrated the home and shaped its sexual politics. Our next task is to look more deeply into the culture of competitive self-reliance, to see how it instills a pornographic sensibility in the souls of American men.

4

Pornographic Manhood

BILL MARGOLD, who writes and directs pornographic films, says that most X-rated productions are meant for solitary use by men. "Couples movies" do exist, he admits, and he grudgingly concedes that "some adult films may well be made for women." He mocks the success of Candida Royale, who took the lead in developing a women's market: "She is quite pleased about being a spokeswoman in the Industry. She lectures at colleges about the wonders of porn." Margold insists that the core appeal of pornography is the "catharsis or release" that it provides for "hedonistic hermits": "you grab a video, run home, slam it into your machine, never have to have any contact with anybody else in the world" (Stoller and Levine 21–22).

The fantasies that carry men on this "magic carpet ride" are not about womanly fulfillment. They carry an edge of hostility, depicting women coerced and humiliated, or worse. "I'd like to bring even more violence into my creations," says Margold. "I'd like to bring what I call erotic terror: the stabbing in the shower in *Psycho,* the ax murder in *Dementia 13.* I'd like to really show

what I believe the men want to see: violence against women"
(ibid. 22). Margold complains that shifting public tastes and the
threat of censorship have limited what he can put on the screen.
"The most violent we can get," he says, "is the cum shot in the
face."

These remarks, from a 1993 interview by Robert Stoller, indicate how complex and multifarious the porn industry has become, as producers respond to the fluctuations in social attitudes that shape their markets. The feminist critique of
pornography—led by Susan Brownmiller, Andrea Dworkin, Susan Griffin, Catherine MacKinnon, Joan Hoff, Susan Gubar,
and Robin West and elaborated by dozens of other writers—
enters Margold's calculations, as does the threat of government
censorship, now vigorously endorsed by the religious right.
Likewise audible are the enthusiasms of pro-porn feminists like
Laura Kipnis and Lisa Palac, who argue that sexually explicit
material enlarges the domain of sexual autonomy and self-realization for women. The legal and ethical issues surrounding the
production and marketing of pornography, like those at stake
in defining it, now form the subject of a complex debate. But
Margold's core contention remains incontestable: porn routinely—if not always—intimates violence against women, or explicitly portrays it, because men find "catharsis" in seeing it.
Consumption of pornographic violence provides "release" for a
furtive and guilt-stricken psychological craving in which sexual
desire is fused with the impulse to subordinate and degrade
women.[1]

Margold's preferred genre of abusive pornography originated
in the early nineteenth century to serve the genre of manhood

then becoming canonical. It is a literature responsive to consternations of sexual experience that are endemic to competitive self-reliance. Hard, isolate, and stoic individualism builds the war of the sexes into the definition of manhood, and into the experience of men, producing a chronic scenario of auto-aggression that is autoerotic. Involuntary desire, gendered "feminine," becomes the target of an internal siege carried out to protect and consolidate "manly" selfhood. Nathaniel Hawthorne's *The Scarlet Letter* provides a detailed anatomy of this masculine self-war and the pornographic compulsion that results. Hawthorne's masterpiece dramatizes the conflicted psychosocial structures that took form in the popular culture of his time, as warrior manhood was becoming compulsory for middle-class American men.

In *The Invention of Pornography*, Lynn Hunt observes that the genre is defined collaboratively by those who produce it and those who try to stamp it out. Lists of forbidden titles in prerevolutionary France include erotic books—like *Thérèse Philosophe*—mingled together with the general run of items deemed treasonable and seditious: attacks on the *ancien régime* frequently accused clerics and great lords of sexual depravity, offering graphic descriptions of their lewd behavior. Robert Darnton has noted that, far from feeling implicated in the vices they portrayed, the social critics who produced this body of satire used it to deliberate the prospects and dilemmas of revolution and to scoff at the sterile frivolity of the old order.

The Marquis de Sade defended the traditional sexual prerogatives of the aristocracy in defiance of the rising democratic ethos, and heralded the spiritual benefits of sexual cruelty in a cultivated literary style that asserts upper-class privilege. This strand of sexually violent writing has descendants in our own time, notably *The Story of O,* and it has acquired elite defenders in the literary academy and elsewhere, who share its contempt for the now-dominant tradition of middle-class morality.

A century before de Sade, however, the Virginia gentleman William Byrd II recounted his sexual exploits in a private diary that bears scant evidence of such resentment or guilt. "About seven I went to Mrs. FitzHerbert's," begins a typical entry. "About nine I walked away and picked up a girl whom I carried to the bagnio and rogered her twice very well. It rained abundance in the night" (Fischer 301). Byrd copulated with "relatives, neighbors, casual acquaintances, strangers, prostitutes, the wives of best friends, and servants both black and white" (ibid. 300); he probably exercised patrician entitlements more energetically than did most men of his class, and his example contrasts sharply with the sexual folkways of that time in Puritan New England, where women enjoyed stronger protections. But even in New England men born to gentry status enjoyed sexual privileges that became abhorrent as the influence of democratic values grew stronger.

A cry went up in America's early national period against the "gay leaders of fashionable life" who ensnared young women and ruined their lives. Susanna Rowson's *Charlotte Temple* and Hannah Foster's *The Coquette* were bestselling American novels of the 1790s that portrayed the wretchedness of women seduced and abandoned by upper-class rakes. The "lovely daughters of America," declared one writer in 1837, must beware of devoting their "pure affections to the polluted wretch, who deserves the names of libertine and seducer" ("Seduction" 162).

Early nineteenth-century American pornography lacks the ethical self-confidence of sexually predatory aristocrats and their prerevolutionary critics, even when it espouses social reform. Rather than jeering at the vices of decadent lords and clergy, the reader of the new porn found himself inveigled into the mingled desire and guilt of sexual aggressors alarmingly like himself. In the writings of George Lippard, George Thompson, and John Neal the portrayal of sexual vice takes on a prurient life of its own. Rather than attacking social evils that are rendered as a distinct target, this literature implicates the reader in the sexual misconduct represented, and an alarming vein of cruelty runs through the experience of contaminated involvement. Surveying the erotic writing of the 1840s, David Reynolds finds it marked by a "unique combination of prurient sexuality and grisly gore" (212). Karen Halttunen has demonstrated that this new public appetite shaped the depiction of murder cases in the news media, which now showcased sexual murders and placed a distinctive new emphasis on what she terms "the pornography of violence" (60).

The term "pornography" entered the English language in 1850 and was quickly applied to the new mode of sexual writing (Kendrick 1–32). Twentieth-century definitions, like contemporary instances, often retain qualities first observed in the antebellum period. The standard adopted by the U.S. Supreme

Court in 1966 specifies material that "appeals to the prurient interest," implying an itch that gets worse as it is scratched ("Regulation" 308). "Prurient," according to the *Oxford English Dictionary*, originally referred to any persistent desire or craving, as in a "prurient longing after . . . personal gossip"; but such uses are now rare, displaced by the tar-baby effect of middle-class smut. Consuming porn heightens the impulse to consume porn, so the definition affirms; and this experience carries forward the quality of the guilty and obsessive reader involvement that became characteristic of the genre in the early nineteenth century. The pornographic manhood served by this literature takes form—then as now—in the sexual politics of the middle class home.

———

The domestic ideal taught that sex between husband and wife conveyed the spiritual communion that bound them together in marriage. Here their complementary biological natures formed a physical union that consecrated the union of their souls. Erotic relations became "personal" in this new marital convention; the term "intercourse" was transferred from its earlier applications to diplomacy and commerce and came to signify coitus as a mutual exchange. By the end of the nineteenth century, "sexuality" had been coined to express this item of social faith, that erotic experience conveys and embodies personhood.

The worldly warrior did not, however, lay aside the anxious self-reliance that is demanded by capitalist economic competition and political strife when he came home.[2] On the contrary, he expected his home to confirm and reward his manly virtue while mollifying the injuries he had received in exercising it. Marital sexuality expressed his manhood when it gave him a position of self-control and uncompromised initiative, which meant that his wife must adopt a womanhood from which active desire was excluded. Before the early nineteenth century women were generally deemed more sexually ardent than men; the domestic ideal implanted the opposite view, that of true women as "passionless."

Ralph Waldo Emerson captured the defining feature of self-reliant male spirituality when he declared that "nothing is sacred except the integrity of your own mind" (149). Yet this integrity is desecrated when the mind is swamped by unwelcome desire. Only when a man monopolizes the initiative does he exercise self-command in sexual relations. If an "impure" woman seeks to arouse him sexually, she simultaneously arouses his contempt and becomes a suitable target for rape. Coercing her has the effect of cleansing him, washing away the pollution entailed by his loss of command. The domestic angel, in contrast, is stainless and pure, offering her husband redemption as she yields to his unilateral advances.

These psychic complexities of middle-class manhood were reinforced by economic imperatives that penetrated the presumptive sanctuary of the home. The economic value of children was radically transformed when industrialization moved economic productivity outside the household and fathers left home to make a living. In colonial America, tradesmen headed households that carried on profitable work, and children were an asset in the cooperage, or the smithy, or the carpenter's shop, as they were on the family farm. After a few years children could be put to work, and they learned the trade growing up. But in the new economy, children became an expense and usually required schooling outside the home to acquire the skills necessary for maintaining middle-class status. As this scheme of things reorganized the social landscape, large families were no longer a sign of prosperity: excessive childbearing, like excessive drinking, became a well-recognized harbinger of ruin.

The result was a striking reduction in the birthrate. Between 1800 and 1850 the average number of children born to white women fell 23 percent, from 7.04 to 5.42; it fell to 3.56 by 1900 (Degler 181). Behind these numbers lies a revolution in the sexual interaction of husbands and wives. Until late in the century reliable contraceptives were unavailable, as was the knowledge required for the "rhythm method." The only dependable strategy for preventing conception was marital abstinence. After the joys of the honeymoon, when the first child was often conceived, sex between married couples was strictly self-policed.

In his classic study of manhood in the nineteenth century, G. J. Barker-Benfield termed the resultant ethos a "spermatic economy," in which a man could bankrupt himself psychologically by "spending" too much semen. Economic pressures reinforced the psychic requirements that compelled a worldly warrior to insist on "purity" as the defining virtue of womanhood. The stainless innocence fitting a woman for marriage reassured a man that she would not provoke him into ruining their finances via unwanted childbirth.

The momentous social power of the angel/whore dichotomy arises from its origins in this male sexuality of anxious self-control. As a "pure" woman seconds masculine command, so ungoverned passion is projected onto her "fallen" sister. The split womanhood imposed on women by this convention arises from a manhood likewise split, between an avowed "masculine" self that retains sexual self-possession and a disavowed "feminine" self that suffers involuntary desire. Actual women are recruiting into performing the ungoverned arousal that men do not acknowledge as their own, and are then held responsible for having provoked it. This pornographic scenario is central to the emerging genre of illicit writing.

George Lippard's *The Quaker City* provides a classic instance of the new porn. Lorrimer and Mary sit on a sofa in the Rose Chamber of Monk Hall, a gothic castle of lust in downtown Philadelphia. The two figures appear to be perfect opposites: Lorrimer is an experienced sexual predator, Mary an innocent maiden. "It was the purpose of this libertine," Lippard writes, "to dishonor the stainless girl, before he left her presence. Before daybreak she would be a polluted thing." Mary in this scenario is evidently a woman, soon to be raped by a man, namely Lorrimer. Yet "Mary" is, in effect, a man in disguise.

As Susan Griffin observes in *Pornography and Silence*, male dominance controls the pornographic script by defining its leading figures in such a way as to conceal the underlying transaction (39). Lorrimer and Mary play out the sexual predicament of self-divided manhood, giving to "Mary" the sexual vulnera-bility that constitutionally self-commanding men cannot ac-knowledge in themselves. This subsurface logic gives coherence and force to an interaction that is ludicrously implausible on its face.

Lorrimer plans to seduce Mary by describing a romantic landscape in Wyoming, confident that she won't realize that lust has overpowered her until she is too far gone to resist. Lorrimer—the "man"—embodies deliberate rational scheming; Mary is devoid of self-awareness, a vessel of involuntary pas-sion. "While enchaining the mind of the Maiden, with a story full of Romance, it was his intention to wake her animal nature into full action. And when her veins were all alive with fiery pul-sations, when her heart grew animate with sensual life, when her eyes swam in the humid moisture of passion, then she would sink helplessly into his arms, and—like the bird to the snake—flutter to her ruin" (127).

Notice the repetitive phrases, meant to solicit the reader's en-gagement in Lorrimer's lust, a rhetoric Lippard advances by punctuating the long-winded description of the Wyoming landscape with snapshots of Mary's breasts being pushed out of her robe by accelerated panting. As the male reader enters this imaginative schema, he becomes two: identifying with the crafty manipulations of the man, he covertly identifies with the abject passion of the woman. The figure of Lorrimer offers a se-cure vantage point from which the reader observes—and yields to—the fascinating loss of self-awareness and self-command suffered by Mary. "Fixing his gaze upon her blue eyes, humid with moisture, he slowly flung back the night robe from her shoulders. Her bosom, in all its richness of outline, heaving and throbbing with that long pulsation, which urged it upward like a billow, lay open to his gaze" (132).

Such portraits of the quarry—paralyzed and throbbing under the eye of the predator—are ubiquitous in *The Quaker City*. Innocent maidens, as well as their polluted sisters, are pictured alluringly asleep or drugged with passion, recapitulating the scenario in which a male aggressor, cynical and resolute, masters the helpless damsel.

Yet as the rapist takes control of his victim, he loses control of himself. The passion masquerading as "Mary's" suddenly erupts within Lorrimer, and he becomes "a fearful picture of incarnate LUST." Lorrimer becomes the phallus, not as commanding, but as surrendering to the ungovernable forces erupting within the phallus itself. "His face grew purple, and the veins of his eyes filled with thick red blood. He trembled . . . and his chest heaved and throbbed beneath his white vest, as though he found it difficult to breathe . . . Playing with the animal nature of the stainless girl, Lorrimer had aroused the sensual volcano of his own base heart" (132–133).

The pornographic manhood that took form in antebellum America incessantly produces and consumes a fantasy-drama picturing a self-possessed male aggressor and a woman falling victim to her own desire; yet as the male aggressor consummates his triumph, he succumbs to the volcano of lust. Lorrimer rapes Mary, exactly as he intended, but instead of confirming his self-command, the assault propels him into a nightmare of self-loathing. He is transfixed by the sounding of an "Awful Bell" whose "judgment peal" breaks "on the ear of the Criminal . . . with a sound that freezes his blood with horror," announcing "the foul wrong, accomplished in the gaudy Rose Chamber of Monk-hall, by the wretch, who now stood trembling in the darkness" (135).

In the new pornography the abuse of women is linked to male sexual self-hatred, a pattern that also appears in the "male purity" literature that developed in the early nineteenth century. Silly as it appears in retrospect, the quest for "purity" was a widespread preoccupation well into the latter decades of the nineteenth century, featuring the sexual cruelties men inflicted upon themselves along a line of battle that separated manly self-command from effeminate lust. Exponents of male hygiene likened orgasm to the convulsions of acute cholera or heart attack, and warned against the "debilitation" that follows, especially when a man's defenses collapse and his desire propels him into orgasm after orgasm. In the emotional economy of male hygiene, impromptu desire fused with self-loathing, making an amalgam that carried a variety of lurid titles: "excessive lasciviousness," "diseased prurience," "nervous melancholy," and "polluted lassitude" (Nissenbaum 106–108).

The self-war endemic to competitive self-reliant manhood likewise informs the vexations that attached themselves to masturbation, now termed "the solitary vice." Masturbation focused the paradoxes of addictive self-command: it had strong attractions as a nonreproductive and self-initiated form of sexual pleasure, yet it simultaneously entailed a yielding to involuntary passion. This male autoeroticism was anything but carefree; it had sexual cruelty at its heart. The forefathers of Bill Margold's "hedonistic hermits" gratified and punished themselves by reading works like *The Quaker City*. In the literature of masturbation phobia, the attack by the "masculine" against the "feminine" component of the male self takes form as an exchange between the victim of self-abuse and the physician who proposes to cure him.

"My constitution," says the masturbator, "is broken down, and my mind, as well as body, completely enervated. I am haunted day and night with lascivious thoughts and dreams; suspicious of my friends and disgusted with my self. My memory has lost its power—unable to fix my attentions—my mind is filled with terrible forebodings—fear of insanity, and at times it has cost me a continual effort to retain my reason." The rational and authoritative physician finds evidence here of an inexorable logic: the victim is diseased because he has violated his own nature. "The organic law of our formation is imperative and abiding," he declares, "no abuse of it will go unpunished" (Rosenberg and Smith-Rosenberg 10).

Like Lorrimer and Mary, the two figures that organize the literature of masturbation phobia are gendered male and female: the physician speaks for self-command; the victim of self-abuse embodies a pitiable form of womanhood, which results when manhood collapses into its opposite. The violence interior to warrior manhood is thus an autoerotic violence; it marks as "womanly" enduring male impulses—here sexual impulses—and singles them out for attack. The sexes themselves are defined as incompatible opposites through this inner violence, and the gestures through which this violence exerts itself carry an erotic charge.

The more severe remedies for masturbation carried an unmistakable note of erotic preoccupation and the quest for sadistic satisfaction. One expert advised that the self-abuser be placed in a straitjacket with his feet tied apart, so his penis would not be tickled by his thighs. The "genital cage" was invented to contain the penis and scrotum; leeches were applied, as well as heated pneumatic cups, to draw off "congestion." Inserting a metal ring in the genitals was a form of treatment, as was the application of caustic chemicals to make the genitals painful to touch (Haller and Haller 208–209).

The Scarlet Letter has been celebrated as a classic since its publication in 1850. It is now read more widely in schools and colleges than any other work of American literature, and it has been presented in multiple versions on stage and screen. Like the white whale, the scarlet letter has entered common parlance; the term is applied to sports heroes, clergymen, and politicians, as well as to AIDS victims, when public dramas of shaming take on a life of their own, soiling accusers along with the accused. America is still a nation "where iniquity is dragged out into the sunshine" (54), with morally ambiguous results.

In *Dearest Beloved* I argued that Chillingworth and Dimmesdale embody the masculine and feminine components of an autophobic middle-class sexuality (184–198). This sexuality is also auto-aggressive: the relation of "masculine" to "feminine" as enacted by these two male figures is sexually violent, and the manhood they represent is pornographic. In *The Scarlet Letter* Hawthorne's "catlike faculty of seeing in the dark" (James 502) sees through Lippard's conventional scenario to examine the intramale drama that secretly informs and propels it.

The story begins with the eroticized punishment of Hester, exposed to public view as the living emblem of sexual sin. Having stitched the "A" with "fertility and gorgeous luxuriance of fancy" (53), Hester attempts to defy the communal assault, but her gesture of refusal is taken as a provocation and has the effect of magnifying the gratification that the scene provides to those who have gathered to view her punishment. The book opens, that is, with a scene of pornographic excitement, at the end of which she is led back to prison hysterical with agony.

This emotional rape is gendered male-on-female even when those who seek pleasure from it are female. Around the foot of the scaffold, Hawthorne tells us, stand "man-like" women who insist that Hester should suffer a harsher and more gratifying penalty. "'It were well,' muttered the most iron visaged of the old dames, 'if we stripped Madam Hester's rich gown off her dainty shoulders'" (54).

Hester's role in the erotic life of the community is indicated by the ardent demand for her needlework. She is hired to produce fine dresses for fine ladies and rich gowns for men of state.

She becomes a celebrity, a precursor of the sex goddesses and sex workers in contemporary America, who cater to a sensibility in which sexual excitement is intercut with vengeance and shame. Yet in keeping with the angel/whore dichotomy, she is never hired "to embroider the white veil which was to cover the pure blushes of a bride" (83). A community-wide transaction springs to life every time she passes along the streets, inspiring guilt and rage because she provokes a desire that is felt as contaminating.

The Scarlet Letter draws the reader into a hall of mirrors that endlessly replicates the intramale drama of masculine-on-feminine sexual cruelty. Consider the emotional life of Hester's remorseful lover, Arthur Dimmesdale. The target of Arthur's self-torture is female, namely his own liability to runaway emotion, including runaway desire. Dimmesdale too becomes a sexual celebrity, inaugurating a tradition of preacher-seducers that runs through Henry Ward Beecher to Elmer Gantry to Jimmy Swaggart, public men who possess a charisma whose erotic power remains intact only so long as it remains invisible to the public. The torments of sexual guilt sound through Arthur's preaching and form the major reason for its hypnotic power. Because his displays of conscientious suffering are also covert exhibitions of desire, he arouses an unconscious reciprocal desire in his parishioners. The more Dimmesdale loathes himself, the more famous he becomes.

Arthur has professional reasons for cultivating his emotional pain, but he also derives intimate satisfaction from the access it gives him to sexual passion. The violence that the "manly" Arthur brings against the "womanly" Arthur is autoerotic, it is a self-rape. He lashes himself into a frenzy of loathing, which is also a frenzy of arousal. "In Mr. Dimmesdale's secret closet, under lock and key, there was a bloody scourge. Oftentimes . . . [he] had plied it on his own shoulders; laughing bitterly at himself the while, and smiting so much the more pitilessly, because of that bitter laugh" (144).

Roger Chillingworth similarly dramatizes male-on-female sexual violence; his inner torture mirrors Arthur's, with the difference that he does not recognize his torment as his own. Roger cannot control his own compulsive self-control. When he sees his wife Hester on the scaffold, with another man's child in her arms, his emotional convulsion is "so instantaneously controlled by an effort of his will, that, save at a single moment, its expression might have passed for calmness" (61). The passions that ravage the surface of Dimmesdale's life are equally forceful in Roger's life, but are hidden from others and from himself.

Roger makes Arthur Dimmesdale into a "woman," upon whom to project his disavowed emotional torments, and a pornographic enchantment with the troubled clergyman soon overcomes him. Roger proposes to carry out an investigation that will disclose the identity of Hester's lover; but no such investigation occurs. Roger is devoted not to discovering Arthur's guilt but to tantalizing and prodding him so as to enhance it. He gives Arthur poisons that keep him alive and keep him in pain.

Roger and Arthur are enmeshed in the same obsession. Roger's torture of Arthur and Arthur's self-torture are versions of the same intramasculine male-on-female assault, and they equally contribute to the lesion that appears on Arthur's chest.

Hawthorne invokes the rhythms of sexual climax in the moment when Roger invades most fully the intimacy of his feminine double, but not the rhythms of a sexuality at home with itself. What Roger experiences is the convulsive and dismaying loss of control that George Lippard depicts in Lorrimer's triumph. It is an orgasm experienced as polluting, "a ghastly rapture . . . bursting forth through the whole ugliness of his figure," which comes upon Roger as he—again like Lorrimer—lays his hand on Arthur's "bosom" and "thrusts aside" the robe that covers it. Roger then feasts his eyes on the core emblem through which Hawthorne explores the psychology of pornographic manhood. The scarlet letter on Arthur's breast was collaboratively produced by the sexualized hatred that Roger feels for Arthur and that Arthur feels for himself.

When Arthur bares his chest at the conclusion of the narrative, the ostensible logic of the moment says that justice has triumphed, because Arthur has a copy of Hester's letter seared into his flesh; but there is a deeper logic saying the reverse.

Hester's letter is a copy of Arthur's. Her public designation as a "fallen" woman is a gesture of the manhood at work in Arthur's self-torture, in Chillingworth's vengeance, and in the community at large. The punishment Hester suffers and the brand she wears are the outward and visible sign of a masculine spiritual pathology that remains secretive and inward. Hawthorne intimates this reverse logic, though he does not spell it out. Arthur pulls open his shirt in a chapter entitled "The Revelation of the Scarlet Letter," as though the letter had never before been revealed. The letter on Hester's breast was merely a phantom, not the real thing at all, but only its product and reflection. As Dimmesdale himself proclaims, "Hester's Scarlet Letter . . . with all its mysterious horror . . . is but the shadow of what he bears on his own breast" (255).[3]

The Scarlet Letter depicts a society dominated by pornographic manhood, with an endemic sexual violence that draws women into its invisible logic. Yet in Hester Prynne Hawthorne dramatizes the struggle of women to disentangle themselves from this enslavement, to find lives of independent self-respect, and to define an autonomous sexual selfhood. The doctrine that the "nature" of women subordinates them to men, like the "angel/ whore" fantasy, aided the effort to maintain traditional male dominance in an American society that had embraced ideals of democratic equality. But a prophetic minority of women challenged the massive political and economic disabilities of women and sought equality with men.

In 1848, two years before Hawthorne published *The Scarlet Letter*, the Women's Rights Convention at Seneca Falls, New York, adopted a "Declaration of Rights and Sentiments" modeled directly on the Declaration of Independence and setting forth a charter for women's liberation based on a radical reinterpretation of "natural" rights (Griffith 54). The character of Hester Prynne is modeled on Margaret Fuller, whom Hawthorne knew well, the most intellectually powerful feminist of the antebellum period. Fuller's *Woman in the Nineteenth Century* (1845) likewise set out a charter of freedom, declaring that women should be empowered to fashion a new womanhood founded on the experiences that would develop once they were liberated from conventions of male dominance.

Hawthorne invokes Fuller and Seneca Falls when he states that Hester's ostracism gave her a spiritual independence in which "the world's law was no law for her mind." Hester is appalled by the pervasive injustices women suffer and the huge effort required to correct them:

> As a first step, the whole system of society is to be torn down, and built up anew. Then, the very nature of the opposite sex, or its long hereditary habit, which has become like nature, is to be essentially modified, before woman can be allowed to assume what seems a fair and suitable position. Finally, all other difficulties being obviated, woman cannot take advantage of these preliminary reforms, until she herself shall have undergone a still mightier change; in which perhaps, the etherial essence, wherein she has her truest life, will be found to have evaporated. (165–166)

Hawthorne gives Hester this speech in order to subvert her claim—and that of nineteenth-century feminists—to democratic equality. At the end of the narrative Hester still believes that "the whole relation of man and woman" needs to be placed "on a surer ground of mutual happiness," but has concluded that she herself is "too stained with sin" to bring in the new order. Instead, she declares, "the angel and apostle of the coming revelation must be a women, indeed, but lofty, pure, and beautiful." As Hester invokes the angel/whore dichotomy against her own moral authority, Hawthorne confirms the male-dominant definitions of gender that his society was busily constructing.

Yet the deep imaginative power of Hawthorne's narrative lies not in its ostensible message but in its unresolved conflicts. The defeat of Hester's revolutionary vision stands permanently in opposition to the victorious strength with which Hawthorne enunciates it. Hawthorne's ambivalence about Hester splits his representation of her along the fault line that divides American sexual culture against itself. We found the same pattern in Whitman's paradox, women celebrated as autonomous and self-respecting individuals, yet sexually subordinated by men. Hawthorne meant for Hester to stand as a warning against womanly independence, but also as a figure of heroic defiance against gender conventions to which Hawthorne himself submitted very unwillingly.

At the moment of her strongest rebellion, Hester represents a marginalized voice of the 1850s, but a voice that was destined to persist, to win social changes across a broad range of legal and economic issues, and to insist in our own time on democratic equality in sexual relations. And Hester was right to foresee that the "nature" of men and the "etherial essence" of women must undergo mighty changes before the autonomy of women becomes a standard that shapes the relations of women and men, especially their sexual relations.

Men need to repudiate the manhood that dooms us to pornographic enchantments and cripples our capacity for egalitarian intimacy with women. Dimmesdale and Chillingworth die as victims of this self-divided manhood; but Hester lives on as a figure of the courage required to envision—and to undertake—the task of building democratic relations between women and men. Yet nearly a century passed, following the publication of *The Scarlet Letter,* before literary scholars began to recognize Hester as a source of feminist inspiration. The ideology of male dominance with which Hawthorne surrounds her took the foreground, screening the radical exploration of gender injustice that the work provides. Unearthing such tacit meanings has been a task for our own time, a task that must continue to move forward. Men seeking to construct democratic masculinities should likewise find inspiration in the courage Hawthorne portrays in Hester.

5

Investigations behind the Veil

Alfred Hitchcock's *Psycho* was an overnight smash hit and soon took a place among America's film classics. Audiences were shocked by Hitchcock's violation of long-standing taboos against the representation of sexual violence, yet they were also thrilled. The film flouted prohibitions that were ready to collapse, and revealed forbidden realities that audiences were eager to see. This is true in part because the murder of Marion Crane by Norman Bates is explained in terms that make men safe. The young woman—symbolically washing away her sexual sin—is slain by the knife-wielding maniac because the maniac has a problem with his mother. Marion's death expiates her own sexual transgression, but it also expiates the tyranny of women over men. Norman is a plaything of womanly forces: feminine power controls his conscience, in deadly conflict with feminine power controlling his desire.

The appetite for depictions of sexual violence is fickle because anxieties must be placated when that appetite is gratified.

Certain violations of taboo successfully negotiate the battle-ground of attraction-plus-distress; others encounter a solid wall of aversion.

As *Psycho* was making Hitchcock famous, *Peeping Tom* wrecked the career of Michael Powell. Powell was more re-spected than Hitchcock in 1960, when both films were released, and Powell's film of sexual murder is substantially less graphic than *Psycho*. Yet the film critic Derek Hill voiced a consensus when he wrote that "the only really satisfactory way to dispose of *Peeping Tom* would be to shovel it up and flush it swiftly down the sewer." The male protagonist of *Peeping Tom* is a shy young man named Mark, who carries a movie camera everywhere he goes. Instead of living in his mother's house, like Norman Bates, Mark lives in the house of his father.

The core image of *Peeping Tom* is screened at the outset. It is the face of a prostitute who is looking into Mark's camera, at first provocatively, then in surprise, then in fear, then with ter-ror that grows until the filming stops. Mark's procedure for killing his victims follows the corresponding steps: he films her as she seeks to arouse him sexually, then as she sees a knife blade protruding from one leg of his tripod and realizes that he intends to kill her, and finally as she witnesses her own death in a mirror he has attached to the camera, which shows her the image of her face.

Why does Mark commit murders in order to produce this scenario, of women terrorized by the sight of their own terror? Why does he want to film it? *Peeping Tom* answers that Mark makes the women into an image of his own inner terror, and that his program of serial killing is his effort to stare that terror down.

Mark's father was an experimental psychologist who used Mark for research into the effects of extreme fear, and in adulthood Mark replays films that capture his boyhood distress, to the tune of uncontrollable screaming, moaning, and sobbing. Mark suffers an extreme version of the cruelty that fathers—and surrogate fathers like coaches and drill sergeants—expect their charges to withstand.

Powell thus traces male sexual violence to its origins in the socialization that makes boys into men, and the audiences of 1960 were disgusted. Viewing sexual violence as the consequence of mothering felt deliciously wicked; that it results from fathering was rubbish, to be flushed down the sewer.

The dilemmas that convulse our experience are not abolished merely because they are exiled from awareness. Unutterable truths live on silently, printing their shape on the patterns of our daily living and entering the imagery of our dreams. Artists of powerful imagination find their way through this dark logic and render it in literary works of singular prophetic acumen. The nightmare vision of *Peeping Tom,* after all, is now being articulated in a new understanding of male socialization.

Uncle Tom's Cabin and *Native Son*—like *Psycho*—were greeted with shock and swiftly gained widespread fame. These novels exposed the horrors of southern slavery and of black oppression in urban ghettos, real horrors urgently needing exposure, and they found large audiences that were eager for accounts of the cruelty and degradation inflicted by whites on blacks.

Yet these works also pursue themes that readers found repugnant: Harriet Beecher Stowe explores the marital rape of white women, and Richard Wright depicts the rapist manhood of white men. Stowe and Wright were appalled and fascinated by the sexual violence endemic to middle-class white society, and they explored these issues overtly in works that are forgotten today. Like *Peeping Tom,* Stowe's "True Story of Lady Byron's Life" and Wright's *Savage Holiday* aroused vehement disgust.

Uncle Tom's Cabin and *Native Son* conceal their treatment of sexual violation behind a veil; focusing on racial injustice, they investigate cruelties of gender, analyzing miseries still suffered by women, inflicted by men, and suffered by men. Stowe and Wright move beyond the insights offered by *The Scarlet Letter* because they explore the relation of sexual violence to systems of social injustice, in particular the male privilege that denies financial autonomy to women, the class privilege that is sustained by the exploitation of African Americans, and the racial oppression that makes the experience of blacks a screen on which whites project sexual cruelties they prefer not to recognize in themselves.

Stowe confronted the issue of marital rape as she struggled with the public role offered to women in the new democracy, that of shaping political life through their power within the home. As the survival of the republic depended on a morally competent citizenry, so it depended on the mother who encouraged her husband to obey his moral compass amid the tempest of worldly competition, and installed such a compass in her sons. This theory of "republican motherhood" was articulated most energetically by Harriet's sister, Catharine Beecher, whose *Domestic Economy* contained practical advice on the duties of household management and childrearing.

Yet Catharine Beecher never undertook these duties herself. She remained single and pursued a vigorous career that would not have been possible had she married. As the daughter of Lyman Beecher, a famous religious leader, Catharine enjoyed ready access to a national platform on which to exercise her remarkable abilities. For her, motherhood would have been not an avenue toward public achievement but a trap.

The Beecher clan reckoned Harriet would be an "old maid" like Catharine, making as fine a career of the celibate life. In 1835 she chose instead to marry Calvin Stowe, but she cried herself to sleep night after night as the ceremony approached. "About half an hour more" she wrote on her wedding day, and "[I] will cease to be Hatty Beecher and change to nobody knows who . . . I have been dreading and dreading the time" (Hedrick 99).

Stowe's biographer Joan Hedrick notes that Stowe's troubles were not aberrant; on the contrary, she dreaded a marital servitude that was borne by middle-class women generally. The private diaries and correspondence of this era abundantly record the "trembling" of women about to marry, and they had good reason to be anxious. In denouncing southern slavery in *Uncle*

Tom's Cabin, Stowe tacitly invoked a tradition of protest that likened the civil status of wives to that of slaves.

In 1837 Thomas Herttell placed a bill before the New York assembly asserting that the common law of marriage violated rights guaranteed by the Constitution. The doctrine of "coverture," under which a married woman's legal existence was absorbed into that of her husband, deprived her of "her liberty and her property," denied her the power to seek redress in court, and granted her husband "nearly unlimited authority over her person," which included the sexual use of her body. For Herttell a wife resembled a "negro-wench slave" that her husband could not sell (Basch 118).

The legal disabilities of coverture were challenged during the nineteenth century on a number of fronts, and coercive marital sex was identified early as an urgent problem: "How many so called wives," wrote Sarah Grimké in 1838, "rise in the morning oppressed with a sense of degradation, from the fact that their chastity has been violated" (151). Yet feminists were hampered in their efforts to address this issue, because candor like Grimké's was condemned as a violation of feminine propriety. Sexual abuse within marriage was unspeakable, and was therefore protected: opposition had to be smuggled into other causes.

The temperance movement was animated by this impulse, and by 1850 fourteen states accepted "habitual drunkenness" as grounds for divorce, because it encouraged "coarse, beastly, and disgusting" behavior (Isenberg 158, 162). The "closest intimacy" of marriage was polluted, so the argument ran, by the "repulsive condition" of the drunkard husband (ibid. 158–159). Yet jurists were obdurate when the issue of sexual violence became explicit, treating it as "a natural condition of marriage." Legal doctrine rendered marital rape a virtual contradiction in terms. "Throughout the nineteenth century," Nancy Isenberg observes, "no court recognized marital rape as grounds for separation or divorce" (162). Only in the 1970s—half a century after women's suffrage—did legal reform in this area gain significant ground.

Stowe took up the sexual subjugation of married women in "The True Story of Lady Byron's Life," where she sought to reveal "the abyss of infamy which [Lady Byron's] marriage was expected to cover" (Hedrick 357). Lord Byron's affair with his half-sister Augusta Leigh forced his wife into complicity. She bore an obligation to keep silence in the face of her own revulsion, and to maintain a marriage that perpetuated the denial even as the rumors proliferated. "The position of a married woman," Stowe observed, is "similar to that of the negro slave" (360), subject to violation by her husband's sexual misconduct. Stowe was unwilling to be identified with the feminist minority, led by Elizabeth Cady Stanton, who announced at the Tenth National Women's Rights Convention in 1860 that "our present false marriage relation . . . is nothing more or less than legalized prostitution" (Griffith 103). Yet as she denounced Lord Byron's misconduct, Stowe spoke from a root of bitterness in her own experience: the true target of Stowe's protest was the sexual slavery of American women in conventional marriages, not the incestuous husbands of British aristocrats. Stowe's essay was quickly buried under an avalanche of public disgust. Even if the "disgusting," "revolting," "obscene" story was true, her critics declared, Stowe "should not have stained herself" by recounting it (Hedrick, 363).

After the birth of her third child, Stowe acquired an additional servant so as to make time for writing. "I have determined not to be a mere domestic slave," she explained to a friend. "I mean to have money enough to have my house kept in the best manner & yet to have time for reflection" (Hedrick 119). Stowe faced a dilemma that still troubles feminist theory; in order to pursue her professional fulfillment she was obliged to employ other women to carry the domestic burden. This paradox was sharply intensified when Stowe took into her Cincinnati household a "colored girl" whom she obtained across the river in Kentucky, where slave owners offered domestic labor for hire (Hedrick 119).

The clergy, the legal profession, and college teaching were closed to Stowe. The cottage industry of writing offered substantial opportunities, but only if she also bore responsibility for running the household and put her husband's career ahead of her own. Stowe did not employ slave labor out of personal callousness, but to counteract her own servitude under economic arrangements she was not in a position to alter.

Calvin was a sexually importunate husband, so that Stowe's financial difficulties were harshened by a more intimate servitude. She bore twins nine months after the marriage and conceived a third child seven months after giving birth. "I hope

[she] will live through this first tug of matrimonial warfare," her sister Catharine wrote. "She says she shall not have any more children *she knows certain* for *one while*—How she found this out I cannot say but she seems quite confident about it" (Hedrick 117). In order to extend the interval between pregnancies, Harriet and Calvin lived apart, arranging separations that consumed roughly half of the first fifteen years of their marriage.

After a miscarriage in 1845, one of several, Stowe became despondent and traveled to Brattleboro, Vermont, to take the "water cure." The Brattleboro spa was a refuge for relatively affluent women, where they could offer one another consolation and spiritual support and take a break from the stresses of male domination (Sklar 184–185). When Calvin visited Harriet at Brattleboro, he was forbidden to have sex with her, and he objected bitterly to "the mean business of sleeping in another bed, another room, and even another house, and being with you as if you were a withered-up old maid sister instead of the wife of my bosom . . . This having the form of marriage and denying the power therof is, to my mind, of all contemptible things the most unutterably contemptible" (Hedrick 178).

Calvin was not a cruel man. He supported Harriet's career, celebrated her eventual triumph, and acquiesced in the arrangements that reduced the danger of pregnancy. Yet the economic and legal structure defining their marriage placed Harriet in bondage. Calvin could wield the "power" of marriage, if he chose, in opposition to Harriet's will. To reply that he refrained from exercising this power is tantamount to conceding that there were considerate slaveowners in the South, as Stowe did concede in *Uncle Tom's Cabin.*

To soften an unjust system through personal kindness is not the same as abolishing slavery altogether. For Calvin to have sex with his wife was not rape, any more than consensual sex with a slave would have been rape, but it took place in a larger context of sexual coercion. Stowe may have gained a respite during her stay at Brattleboro, but nine months after she was reunited with Calvin she bore her sixth child.

Stowe believed that redemption from unjust suffering is gained through ecstatic submission to it, in keeping with the ideal of "true womanhood," which promised that the spiritual power of a woman in the home could overcome the cruelties of a sinful world. At the core of this doctrine lay the analogy between feminine virtue and the redemptive suffering of Christ on the cross; and as Stowe brooded over her intimate miseries, she carried this analogy one further step. She identified Christlike womanhood with the suffering of slaves. Six months after the birth of her seventh and last child—while meditating on the body and blood of Christ at a communion service—Stowe received the vision of a slave being beaten to death. Scarcely able to "restrain the convulsion of tears and sobbings that shook her frame," Stowe returned home, and immediately wrote out the murder of Uncle Tom, whose Christlike submission to unjust suffering promises redemption, not only for African Americans but also for white women confronting the slavery of marriage (*Life* 146).

Uncle Tom's Cabin consistently depicts rape as a degradation inseparable from slavery. The world of the book features the two domains envisioned by the domestic ideal, the male order of politics and money separated from the "woman's sphere" of intimate relations in the home. Slavery entails the forcible invasion of this feminine interior by male power, as humane husbands get into financial difficulty and are compelled to sell off their slaves, and Stowe underscores the erotic violation implicit in this scenario.

At the outset of the narrative, the slave trader Haley is arranging a purchase from Mr. Shelby when Eliza Harris enters the room, to find "the gaze of the strange man fixed upon her in bold and undisguised admiration. Her dress . . . set off to advantage her finely moulded shape . . . [and] did not escape the quick eye of the trader" (45). Multiplying instances build Stowe's case that women in slavery are generically victims of sexual abuse. Marie St. Claire accuses Rosa of being "saucy" and sends the "pretty young quadroon" to be stripped and beaten. "It was the universal custom," Stowe remarks, "to send women and young girls to whipping-houses, to the hands of the lowest of men— men vile enough to make this their profession—there to be subjected to brutal exposure and shameful correction" (460).

Sexual violation grows more explicit as the story reaches its conclusion. Simon Legree pays an extra hundred dollars for Emmeline after passing his "heavy, dirty hand . . . over her neck and bust" (477), and the sexual abuse that is commonplace on Legree's plantation motivates the killing of Uncle Tom. A young woman named Lucy rejects the foreman's sexual demands, and Legree decides that Tom "shall have the pleasure of flogging her" (505); when Tom refuses, the sexual sadism focused on Lucy is transferred to him.

Another victim of Legree's regime is Cassy, whose story details the sexual subjugation of women dominated by the economic power of men. Cassy's white father dies without fulfilling his promise to free her, whereupon she falls in love with the man who inherits her, and bears him two children. But he contracts gambling debts and is forced to sell Cassy (with the children) to a man she dislikes. This new owner forces Cassy into sexual service by threatening to sell off the children, and having secured her compliance, sells them anyway. Soon Cassy hears the screaming of her son as she passes a whipping house, goes berserk with rage, and tries to murder her owner. Eventually purchased by a "kindly" Captain Stuart, who tries to buy back her children so they can all be reunited in his slave quarters, Cassy is not mollified: she kills the son she bears to Captain Stuart, to prevent his growing up a slave. Given the chance, she tells Tom, she would gladly kill Legree as well.

The enduring imaginative power of *Uncle Tom's Cabin* rests largely on Stowe's depiction of the subterranean forces that shaped—and continue to shape—the experience of middle-class women, including Stowe's experience. Harriet's marriage to Calvin was legitimate and freely chosen, but it placed her in a system of subordination that included unwanted sex and unwanted pregnancies, a system resting on the denial to women of fundamental human rights. Stowe herself endorsed the rhetoric of domestic bliss, so that her sexual enslavement and her rage against it were deeply repressed, but they become visible through Cassy.

Tom plays the role of redemptive wife, even as Legree's foremen beat him to death. Trapped in the heartless world of money and power, the murderers are reduced to tears by Tom's loving submission (585). Through Uncle Tom, Stowe celebrates the womanhood suited to a rape culture, in which women fulfill themselves, and redeem their assailants, when they lovingly submit to assault. The claim that Christianity ordains such a role for women has by no means died away; it is audible in the 1998 statement of the Southern Baptist Convention that a wife is obliged to "submit herself graciously" to the "leadership" of her husband. The active force underlying this theology of terror is the politics of gender: as sexual violence became inherent to American manhood, so the submission to sexual violence became inherent to American womanhood.

After publishing *Uncle Tom's Children,* Richard Wright composed *Native Son,* whose protagonist Bigger Thomas murders the daughter of a wealthy white man and incinerates her body in the furnace of her father's house. A more drastic repudiation of the "Uncle Tom" ideal could hardly be imagined. Yet to James Baldwin, Wright's horrific tale was "a complement of that monstrous legend it was written to destroy. Bigger is Uncle Tom's descendant, flesh of his flesh, so exactly opposite a portrait that, when the books are placed together, it seems that the contemporary Negro novelist and the dead New England woman are locked together in a deadly, timeless battle" (22).

Baldwin accused Wright of falling victim to white prejudice, and of shaping Bigger Thomas to match an image of Negro life that white people had concocted. This "American image of the Negro lives also in the Negro's heart" (38), Baldwin argued, luring blacks from faithfulness to their own distinctive traditions. "No American Negro exists," Baldwin declares, "who does not have his private Bigger Thomas living in the skull" (42).

Wright did not deserve this criticism. He explains that Bigger's violence "received its tone and timbre from the strivings of the dominant [white] civilization" (511). The "emotional tensions" at the heart of Bigger's existence, which make him "an American product, a native son of this land" (521), are the result of social arrangements that benefit certain whites and oppress others, Wright declares, so that oppressed whites share the torments that afflict Bigger: "all Bigger Thomases, white and black, [feel] tense, afraid, nervous, hysterical, and restless" (520). But Wright also knew that whites generally, oppressed as well as privileged, cultivate racist fantasies and expect blacks to internalize them.

Wright's narrative explores the complex relationships that link white racism and economic oppression to the gender politics that encompasses white and black men. Bigger Thomas dramatizes the sexual violence inherent to the warrior manhood enshrined in white middle-class culture, just as Stowe's Uncle Tom dramatizes the corresponding ideal of sweet, submissive, and otherworldly womanhood.

The polarity that locks these figures together is the traditional logic of the "opposite" sexes. Yet white Americans have found it convenient to imagine that the destructive features of this gender ideal belong peculiarly to blacks. Black men confront an image of themselves that embodies the nightmare dimensions of white manhood; Wright shapes his narrative to show that Bigger's pursuit of this manhood leads him to live out the nightmare.

The opening scene of *Native Son* dramatizes the manliness that Bigger expects of himself, in relation to a generically terrified womanhood. When a large rat appears on the floor of their ghetto apartment, Bigger's mother and sister scramble whimpering onto the bed, while Bigger kills the rat with a skillet. Then Bigger "laughed and approached the bed with the dangling rat, swinging it to and fro like a pendulum, enjoying his sister's fear" (5).

The rat-killing scene also depicts the social oppression that cheats Bigger of the chance to live out his manhood amid the opportunities available to whites. Bigger does not have a fighting chance in American life; he is a warrior destined for persistent, baffling, and humiliating defeat. The social causes of this situation lie far beyond Bigger's awareness and that of the family in which he seeks to play the man. The Thomases know that they are victims of white oppression, but they don't recognize that a prime feature of this oppression is their subservience to the standard of manhood against which Bigger is certain to fail. "We wouldn't have to live in this garbage dump," his mother accuses Bigger, "if you had any manhood in you" (7).

Wright indicates from the outset that Bigger's cruelty is an effort to manage his own wretchedness by printing it on the faces of his victims. "He hated his family because he knew that they were suffering and that he was powerless to help them. He knew that the moment he allowed himself to feel . . . the shame and misery of their lives, he would be swept out of himself with fear and despair" (9). He enjoys his sister's terror because it forestalls his own.

The "Bigger" psychology in whites and blacks, Wright explains, derives from "primal fear and dread"—"objectless, timeless, spaceless"—a paralyzing anxiety that men may counteract through "rebellion" or "submission and trust" (528). Yet Bigger's society offers him nothing worthy of trust: he despises the pious subservience urged upon him by his mother and by the minister who visits him in his prison cell. Bigger seizes instead the manhood that surmounts terror through violence, and the murder of Mary Dalton provides him relief. "The thought of what he had done, the awful horror of it, the daring associated with such actions, formed for him for the first time in his fear-ridden life a barrier of protection between him and a world he feared. He had murdered and had created a new life for himself" (119).

Bigger's defense attorney describes the class oppression that deprives Bigger of economic opportunity as he seeks to extenuate Bigger's offenses and persuade the court to impose a lighter sentence. Unjustly denied a chance at making a decent life for himself, so the argument runs, Bigger turns to meaningless and self-destructive violence. Wright certainly intends for the reader to accept this interpretation, but not to the exclusion of an alternative view that Bigger himself asserts, namely that violence is the heart of his being, not an aberration. "They wouldn't let me live and I killed . . . When I think of why all the killing was, I begin to feel what I wanted, what I am" (500-501). The killing is not a perversion of Bigger's manhood but confirms it. "What I killed for," he concludes, "I am" (501).

For Bigger, and for Wright, the sexual murders rise directly from the manhood that Bigger yearns to live out within the world of opportunity available to whites. The culture of economic competition instills this manhood in white and black men alike, with the racist proviso that African Americans are made to suffer a crippling handicap. Bigger's sexual violence is the expression of an American manhood that more fortunate native sons—white native sons—live out in the lives they look upon as normal. This logic prompts Bigger to lay claim to a rape he did not commit.

When the white officials determine that Bigger murdered Mary Dalton, they assume he raped her, and the public at large adopts this view once the newspapers give it circulation. Bigger's act is taken up into a public fantasy that falsifies what actually happened; yet Bigger himself shares in this fantasy and affirms the inner truth that it contains. "Had he raped her? Yes, he had raped her. Every time he felt as he felt that night, he raped. Rape was not what one did to women. Rape was what one felt when one's back was against a wall and one had to strike out. It was rape when he cried out in hate deep in his heart as he felt the strain of living day by day" (262-263).

Mary Dalton's first appearance defines her as provender for the rape fantasies by which men sustain their competition with other men. She appears in a movie-house newsreel that Bigger witnesses following a masturbation contest with his friend Jack. This trial of male strength is carried out in the language of combat. "I'm polishing my nightstick," Bigger says, ". . . I wish I had Bessie with me now." To which Jack replies, "I could make old Clara moan now." When a woman walks up the aisle Bigger says, "If she comes back I'll throw it in her." Sex has nothing to do here with love or procreation; it is a quest for hit-man prestige. "You a killer," says Jack admiringly (33).

This scenario frames the social meanings of Mary Dalton, who now appears on screen, a glamorous Chicago debutante on a beach in Florida, "accepting the attentions of a well-known radical." Bigger and Jack understand nothing of radical politics, nor does the intended audience of the newsreel, which is meant to excite the sexual fantasies of a white society that covets the Daltons' fabulous wealth. Mary's relationship to the young radical is conveyed by an image of her legs racing across the sand, chased by his legs. The voice-over comments: "Ha! He's after her! There! He's got her! . . . Ah, the naughty rich" (35). Several dimensions of male-male power are compounded in Mary's being, notably the power of her family's wealth, which co-opts the revolutionary opposition it arouses. The politics of the young radical make him amusing to the rich young lady, as she later finds Bigger amusing.

Class conflict shapes the sexual politics here. Mary is subordinated as an object of male lust, but that lust is aroused in an audience of disempowered males. Like contemporary men who dream of the Playboy Mansion or the penthouse fulfillments of Donald Trump, the customers of the movie house consume the erotic fantasy with little comprehension of the economic situation that ensures their disadvantage, and no means of countering it. The image of the rich white girl is served up to them—as to Bigger and Jack—as a sexual tidbit, suitable for masturbatory fantasies. Male sexuality is thus both served and exploited by the scenario: Mary Dalton is presented as a centerfold, appearing promiscuously available to entice and gratify men. But the men who are aroused by her testify to their own subordination in the moment of arousal.

The male fantasy that Mary Dalton enacts in the newsreel continues when she appears in person, as Wright further dramatizes the theme of male sexual susceptibility as an incarnation of male social victimization. Serving as her chauffeur during a night on the town, Bigger discovers that Mary is too drunk to walk and carries her up to her bedroom, where she embraces him and presses her pelvis against his. Bigger is enraged and terrified by his own arousal, enraged at being toyed with sexually, and enraged at being compelled economically to accept the role of toy. To be caught in a sexual embrace with Mary Dalton would be tantamount to a death sentence, he recognizes, and he kills her to master the consequent terror. The manhood that he asserts in killing her is also asserted in his subsequent claim of having raped her, not as something he had done to a woman, but as something he had done because his back was against the wall.

As he lives out this nightmare, Bigger joins Mary Dalton as a player in the sexual fantasy life of the white majority, who indulge their rapist fantasies through him. The public avidly consumes a brimming tide of news stories, while the police take Bigger back to Mary's bedroom and pressure him to reenact the "rape." "Come on, boy, we've treated you pretty nice ... Get over there by that bed and show us how you raped and murdered that girl! ... Aw come on. What you got to lose now? Show us what you did" (389). This pornographic jamboree reaches its climax in the courtroom.

With a black man in the docket to serve as scapegoat and Mary Dalton defenseless in her grave, the prosecutor elaborates the fantasy in detail:

> How swift and unexpected must have been that lustful and murderous attack! How that poor child must have struggled to escape that maddened ape! How she must have pled on bended knee, with tears in her eyes, to be spared the vile touch of his horrible person! Your Honor, must not this infernal monster have burned her body to destroy evidence of offenses worse than rape? That treacherous beast must have known that if the marks of his teeth were ever seen on the innocent white flesh of her breasts ... (480).

Bigger's rape and murder of his girlfriend Bessie is not of interest to the white public, but Wright's account takes us directly to Bigger's inner experience of the manhood he shares with whites. Bessie is not a rich white girl embodying what frightens him externally, but a poor black girl who serves as a vessel for the powerless fear that threatens to unman him from within. Controlling her and enjoying her sexually allows Bigger to invest her body with his terrors, and deludes him into thinking he can master those terrors by mastering her.

Bessie is unable to play this passive role consistently; she is curious about Bigger's activities and afraid he will get her in trouble. After they have sex, she renews her inquiries and complaints, and Bigger's imagination splits her into discordant parts.

> [He] felt that there were two Bessies: one a body that he
> had just had and wanted badly again; the other was in
> Bessie's face; it asked questions; it bargained and sold
> the other Bessie to advantage. He wished he could . . .
> blot out . . . the Bessie on Bessie's face and leave the
> other helpless and yielding before him. He would then
> gather her up and put her in his chest, his stomach,
> some place deep inside him, always keeping her there
> . . . just to feel and know that she was his to have and
> hold whenever he wanted to. (159–160)

As person in her own right, Bessie is an annoyance; as a prop for his fragile manhood, she is flesh of his flesh and bone of his bone.

Bessie's anxious protests provoke in Bigger an uncanny calm, in which he decides to kill her, "as a man seeing what he must do to save himself and feeling resolved to do it." But Bigger doesn't improve his chances of escape; "as a man" he has fallen prey to a "manly" delusion, thinking he can cancel his inner terrors by assaulting the woman who loves him best, because those terrors speak in her voice. The delusional empowerment that Bigger derives from attacking Bessie reinforces the boost to his morale he acquires by raping her, and the psychological dynamics are the same. What arouses Bigger sexually is what arouses his violence: it is Bessie's helplessness, her "soft" and "piteous" weeping, and then her vain resistance to his onslaught. He hears "a sigh of resignation, a giving up, a surrender of something more than her body . . . His icy fingers touched inside her and at once she spoke, not a word, but a sound that gave forth a meaning of horror accepted" (269–270).

"Rape was not what one did to women" is the falsehood at the heart of Bigger's manhood; "horror accepted" defines the womanhood embodied in Uncle Tom. These fictional black men were created by victims of gender and racial oppression, and they portray the nightmare dimensions of a white manhood that consigns women to service as the repositories of the longing and fear that men abhor in themselves.

Like Harriet Beecher Stowe, Wright knew that the sexual abuses he treated in his masterpiece had deep sources in the political and economic relation of whites with whites, and that the racial injustice suffered by Bigger Thomas only exacerbated, did not fully explain, his compulsive sexual violence. Yet like Stowe, Wright discovered that addressing the pathologies of white manhood directly would bring down public outrage. He pursues the subject in *Savage Holiday,* whose protagonist is Erskine Fowler, a respectable white middle-class businessman, whom we meet at a retirement banquet honoring his many years of service as an insurance company executive. Hidden in this ceremony of privilege, however, lies Fowler's helpless servitude. He was in fact dismissed from his job, to make room for the owner's twenty-three-year-old son. The banquet is a humiliating charade that Fowler cannot muster the courage to repudiate. Instead, he goes through the motions of pride and gratitude, only to strangle on his powerless rage when it's over.

Fowler's self-hatred takes the form of an intense fantasy about female pollution, which he projects into the insurance business, seeing it as "a shifty-eyed, timid, sensual, sluttish woman . . . with all of her revolting sexiness" (28). Fowler next projects this fantasy onto Mabel Blake, who comes to represent the timid whore that the ethos of competitive manhood has made of Fowler himself. Mabel becomes his obsession, a focal point for the desire, hatred, longing, terror, and disgust that churn beneath the orderly surface of Fowler's life, instilled by the terrors of a violent boyhood and his failed effort to find manly self-respect as an adult. The story ends with her sexual murder at his hands. In *Savage Holiday,* the unspeakable is rendered directly; there is no racial issue to shield the reader from a confrontation with the sexual violence of respectable white men. While *Native Son*—like *Uncle Tom's Cabin*—is praised as an American classic, *Savage Holiday* is virtually unknown.

6

Rape as Redemption

THE RAPE MYTH that now captivates the imagination of many American men does not appear in the works of literature we have examined. What we've seen is the historical fashioning of its components: the individualized worldly warfare that splits men into "masculine" and "feminine" opposites, the internal and outward stresses that create systemic conflict across that split, and the pornographic enchantment that temporarily allays the resultant misery.

But the narratives discussed so far surround this transaction with desperation and shame. Lorrimer, Legree, and Bigger Thomas suffer torments of mind, and while Bigger claims that sexual violence anchors his manhood, he does so amid severe distress. These characters do not imagine that women "ask for it" through sexually provocative conduct, and their victims—Mary, Cassy, Bessie—respond with loathing. None reveals a secret desire to be raped.

Norman Mailer's *An American Dream* is a consummate portrayal of the myth. Mailer's celebration of rapist manhood transforms Bigger Thomas—an oppressed ghetto black man—into a model for the spiritual rescue of privileged white men. The logic of this startling reversal can be traced to the gender history that unfolded between the Civil War and World War II, when the advent of modern warfare shattered traditional understandings of warrior virtue and the tradition of self-reliant competitive individualism was reshaped by the culture of corporate capitalism. The fully elaborated modern vision of rapist manhood that Mailer provides did not spring from his imagination alone; it was fashioned in a complex story of American gender and racial bigotry.

Late nineteenth-century Americans confronted a new social order that diminished the opportunities available to whites for exercising individual self-command, and enshrined primordial virility as the remedy. Resurgent primal masculinity promised to rescue manliness from the baffling refinements of advanced civilization. Scenarios of heroic man-to-man combat took center stage in the elaboration of these fantasies, but from the outset there runs a theme of sexual assault. The early expressions of this rapist impulse are covert, and are frequently deflected into African Americans.

A cult of elemental manhood swept white America in the late nineteenth century. The novels of Sir Walter Scott enjoyed a widespread new vogue, proclaiming the virtues of knights-errant who disdain the soft life of the court and travel the forests alone, eager to give battle in defense of imperiled virtue.

Howard Chudacoff describes a new male subculture that arose in barbershops and saloons, where readers of *The Police Gazette* adored John L. Sullivan, the bare-knuckle heavyweight, whose manly exploits in barroom and boxing ring "smashed through the fluff of bourgeois gentility" (241). The body-builder Eugene Sandow, like Harry Houdini and Edgar Rice Burroughs's Tarzan, also served the growing public appetite for spectacles of triumphant muscular virility (Kasson).

Youth organizations formed across American Protestantism that adapted military imagery to the promotion of elemental maleness. Their names invoked a chivalric past: the "Young Crusaders," the "Knights of Temperance," the "Knights of King Arthur." Theodore Roosevelt came to prominence during this epoch, and then to national leadership, as a champion of the strenuous life. The Spanish-American and Philippine-American wars, Kristin Hoganson has shown, were envisioned as salutary exercises for an American culture gone soft. "I should welcome almost any war," Theodore Roosevelt remarked, "for I think this country needs one" (39).

This martial ideal served to counteract a pervasive sense of emasculation in the bourgeois elite. Surrogate forms of combat fed a craving for "real" experience in the midst of a comfortable high-Victorian life that felt stuffy and airless, like a parlor decorated to suit a "feminine" taste. Such compensatory male heroics have been traced to the challenge of feminist activism during this era, when temperance and urban reform movements made gains and voting rights for women were secured in a number of local jurisdictions as the quest for national suffrage pressed forward. But Jackson Lears argues that the root cause of this male malaise lay in the emergence of new economic structures following the Civil War. Lears terms it a "second industrial revolution," with the extension of the railroads across the West as an emblem its nationwide reach. The myth of redemptive rape first took form in this setting.

Here is Lears's summary:

> The second industrial revolution was entwined with the shift from the disorganized entrepreneurial capitalism of the earlier nineteenth century to the organized corporate capitalism of our own time . . . The dominant mode of economic organization was becoming the monopolistic corporation—organized in accordance with precisely calculable and strictly functional procedures, managed by a hierarchical bureaucracy of salaried executives. (9)

The new economic landscape—dominated by huge corporations swiftly replacing a patchwork of local enterprises—altered the terms on which men could seek fulfillment as self-reliant and self-commanding individuals.

White men in antebellum America did not all have equal access to economic opportunity, but the ideal of the autonomous self-made man had enough exemplars to give it material credibility, and the ownership of profit-making establishments provided relative independence for many. This was decreasingly true as business activity was centralized. The great monopolies offered affluence to men capable of submitting to corporate discipline and willing to learn the self-effacement and patience required for professional advancement in a bureaucracy. But such affluence was not control and was not the product of autonomous independent action.

Robert Wiebe explains that early nineteenth-century America established a "fraternity" of white males who shared the opportunities permitting them to make a livelihood by following their own initiative, and who competed on roughly equal terms, while excluding nonwhites and women. But the nationwide corporate order now created hierarchies that separated white men into classes and sharply limited access to autonomous decisionmaking. Newly systematized factory production broke up autonomous work groups that had worked at the direction of "old-style, freewheeling foremen" and depended on multi-skilled persons who could solve problems as they arose. Such teams had been all the more independent because production schedules were intermittent and only these internal "baronies" were capable of gearing down and gearing up production as needed. The new system now demanded continuous production, under protocols that management dictated and that shop-floor workers were compelled to obey. Centralized planning and permanent hierarchy were thus established at the heart of white men's working life, Wiebe observes, and effected a major transition in American social history. "Just as the triumph of self-directed work at the beginning of the nineteenth century undermined the old eighteenth-century hierarchies, so the undermining of self-directed work prepared the way for new hierarchies at the beginning of the twentieth" (156).[1]

But the ideal of manly self-reliance did not die. The self-defined authority instilled in men by antebellum opportunities "gave a grand boost of pride to craftsmen and farmers," Wiebe notes, "many of whom continued to draw energy from those feelings, to define themselves at the heart of American society, even after their autonomy was seriously eroded" (123). Resistance to the new corporate order reached out to a broad base in the early 1880s as Populists denounced "the iron heel of a soulless monopoly, crushing the manhood out of sovereign citizens" (122). But after the Haymarket Square bomb in 1886 the support for unions was sharply reduced, not least because such collective effort seemed alien to the spirit of individual self-reliance.

The powerful new economic and political elite thus consolidated its position by appealing to a vision of democratic fulfillment that was increasingly remote from the experience of ordinary men. As remains true today, discontented men looked to personal "failure" as the reason for their difficulties, rather than challenging monopoly interests. The labor movement remained active, eventually gaining significant power, and new theories in sociology and psychology stressed the collective setting in which personhood takes form. But the large class of professionals, technicians, and managers who served the corporations still accepted the individualist creed, even as that creed was turned against them. They felt ensnared by an "over-civilized" life, believing that the upward march of progress from savagery to ever-higher stages of civilization had cut them off from vital aboriginal roots. This mistaken diagnosis yielded a mistaken prescription: a diet of elemental manliness that was endorsed by national celebrities like Theodore Roosevelt and John L. Sullivan.

Male writers too became icons of manhood, leading a movement that sought to rescue literary culture from the dominance of genteel tastes and feminine idealism. Jack London broadcast his own wilderness exploits—establishing a convention followed by Zane Grey and Ernest Hemingway—so as to confirm the claim that his writings were not conceived in retirement from the rough-and-tumble male world, but right in its midst (see Auerbach). Frank Norris was not so self-dramatizing, but he was enthralled by the new masculinity. His novels explore the social arrangements that produced the cult of primordial manhood and trace out the logic through which redemptive barbarism becomes redemptive rape.

Norris's *The Octopus* chronicles an economic and political battle in which the railroad monopoly destroys an established elite of wheat farmers in California's central valley. Norris celebrates the dignity of these doomed patricians in contrast to the squalid deviousness of the railroad underlings, but at the end of the narrative he brings us face to face with Shelgrim, the president of the railroad, styled as a superman of prodigious intelligence and indomitable will. Laying his huge forefinger on the conference table, Shelgrim declares that he is not personally responsible for the farmers' misery. They were victimized by inexorable economic laws (supply and demand) merged with inexorable natural laws (the cycles of fertility). Shelgrim himself attains titanic stature, over against the little men he has crushed and those he employs, because he embodies both sets of forces. His phallic forefinger signals the incorporation of reproductive potency into the economic power of his monopoly.

Norris scorns the high-society males of San Francisco, who live off the wealth of the great corporations. These "ephemera" adorn their women with luxurious clothing, patronize the art galleries and the opera house, and exhaust their energies between empty well-paid jobs and an endless round of parties. In *Moran of the Lady Letty* Norris dramatizes the redemption of one such feminized sophisticate, Ross Wilbur, who is propelled into manhood when he is shanghaied aboard a shark-hunter that is outward bound through the Golden Gate. When Wilbur dons his smelly oilskins and sniffs the ocean breeze, he feels strangely revived, but the drama of his reborn virility begins in earnest when he encounters Moran.

The only person found alive on a derelict, Moran is brought aboard the shark-hunter semiconscious. When a sudden storm sweeps the captain overboard, threatens to capsize the vessel, and awakens Moran from her coma, she promptly seizes the wheel. "Superb in her wrath at their weakness" (222), Moran shames the paralyzed crew into action. At first Wilbur thinks that this "savage, splendid, dominant" creature is a man, but he soon finds she is a mirror opposite to himself. A master sailor, who grew up at sea with her father, Moran is a manly soul in a woman's body. The two are made for each other, each destined to redeem the other from the gender anomaly to which they have fallen prey. To complete his progress toward manhood, Wilbur must bring out the woman in Moran.

Norris contrives a scene of hand-to-hand combat, precipitated by a pirate attack in which the pair slaughter pirates left and right. Failing to notice that the pirates are all dead, Moran mistakenly attacks Wilbur, and the gender-defining battle is joined. Wilbur fights fiercely, to conquer "her force, her determination, her will, her splendid independence" (287). Moran likewise fights all the harder when she realizes she's fighting Wilbur, eager to test his manhood and find her womanhood in defeat. "You've conquered me . . . [and] I love you for it" (289), Moran says at length, and she yields command of the shark-hunter.

Dominance and submission established by personal violence here define primordial manhood and womanhood. We are not to gather, however, that Moran and Wilbur consummate their newfound identities through sexual intercourse, despite Moran's "complete surrender of herself" (298); in that respect the two remain quite genteel. Only in *McTeague* does Norris add sexual desire to the compound of elemental gender-defining forces.

Unlike the oversophisticated Wilbur, McTeague is a hugely muscular working-class aspirant to middle-class status, trying to make his way as a dentist. Like John L. Sullivan and the other prizefighters and bodybuilders celebrated in the male saloon culture of late nineteenth-century America, McTeague is at once an icon of virility and a brute. He gazes out the window of his Dental Parlor at the fancy ladies shopping on Polk Street with no comprehension of the sources of their wealth. Nor does he understand the social complexities surrounding his daily work. McTeague hopes to purchase a modest home where he can rear children, and he dreams of grandchildren playing around him in his old age. These seem reasonable enough ambitions, since McTeague is a hard-working man with a marketable skill. But he lacks an academic degree, and has no license to practice dentistry. When the municipal authorities demand that he shut down his practice, he is completely disconcerted.

McTeague is faced, that is, with the bureaucratic regulation brought into being by the emergence of the professions in late nineteenth-century America, which transformed the practice of dentistry, as of law and medicine. Rather than a straightforward world in which a competent man can make an honest living at his trade, McTeague confronts the credentialing apparatus of the modern corporate order. Unable to mount a coherent protest against the baffling urban officialdom, McTeague goes out of business and becomes a drunk, sealing his economic doom.

Yet Norris offers McTeague as a figure of titanic maleness, with elemental forces slumbering in his huge powerful body. When a wrestling match arouses him, his customary sluggishness gives way to "the exalted and perverted fury of the Berserker" (133) and he whirls his opponent by the arm like a rag doll. When he bends over the anesthetized body of Trina, a dainty young woman who comes to his Dental Parlor for treatment, primordial sexuality is aroused; he feels "the sudden panther leap of the animal" (18). As McTeague struggles to restrain this predatory instinct, he realizes that ravishing Trina would contaminate her, imprinting her with "the smudge of foul ordure, the footprint of the monster" (18).

The relationship between McTeague and Trina traces out the emerging conventions of an elemental maleness that seizes victims who secretly want to be raped. Lying unconscious on McTeague's dental chair, Trina becomes the object of the "virile desire . . . strong and brutal" that gives McTeague his savage dignity amid the tawdry municipal politics and affluent pretensions of San Francisco's elite. Yet Trina possesses a primal sexuality of which she is unaware, and so the rapist fantasy completes itself. "Crushing down her struggle with his immense strength" McTeague awakens his victim's secret desire: "Trina gave up, all in an instant turning her head to his. They kissed each other, grossly, full in the mouth" (48).

Before the onset of this elemental chemistry Trina had been "without sex," like Moran. But now "the woman within her suddenly awoke" (50), and a flaming passion soon commands her. "Why did she feel the desire, the necessity of being conquered by a superior strength? . . . Why had it suddenly thrilled her from head to foot with a quick, terrifying gust of passion?" (50). Yet for McTeague, Trina's "act of submission . . . made her seem less desirable in his eyes" (51). These contradictory forces drive McTeague and Trina into a marriage, and then destroy it. After the elemental rape that enlivens the wedding night, their sexual relationship quickly degenerates into a saccharine routine, since there remains nothing for McTeague to conquer.

Norris both reveres and abhors the sexual violence inherent in the nineteenth-century cult of primordial virility. He presents McTeague as an awesome figure, who escapes the noxious complexities of city life to die alone in Death Valley, amid vast land forms that—like him—bear the imprint of elemental forces. Yet McTeague is also a pathological brute, contemptible and degraded. McTeague's stupidity, his lower-class status, and his descent into alcoholism combine to place him outside the zone of decent humankind, and there is nothing heroic about his eventual murder of Trina. But Norris provides no savior in *McTeague*, no figure possessing a spiritual force capable of matching that of the rapist hero.

McTeague is a prototype of Bigger Thomas; he embodies the complex of sexually violent impulses that the white society of the Gilded Age projected onto African-American men. From Shakespeare's *Othello* to the O. J. Simpson trial, black men have been assigned leading roles in dramatic enactments of the sexual cruelty that whites do not recognize as their own; in late nineteenth-century America this symbolic violence took concrete form in a new vogue of lynching.

In earlier decades lynching took place mostly on the frontier and its victims were predominantly white. But in the early 1890s, beginning in the South, there arose an epidemic of racist murders justified as revenge for rape. Voicing the widely shared myth, the *New York Times* commented in 1892 that sexual assault is an offense "to which the African race is particularly prone" (Bederman 47). The pioneering activist Ida B. Wells recognized that the lynching of blacks was a scapegoating ritual, noting that the "alleged propensity of black men for raping white women was a myth created to protect the sexual pride of whites" (Harris 16).

In *Exorcising Blackness,* Trudier Harris illuminates further dimensions of the ritual. Believing that blacks are driven by primordial rapist impulses—like those sketched in *McTeague*—white men expiate such impulses by lynching the black men onto whom those desires are projected. But white men simultaneously envy the giant sexuality they imagine black men to possess, because it is a feature of the primal virility they seek to recapture in themselves. In this way, Harris notes, "the white man becomes a victim of his culture's imagination" (20), producing lynch scenarios of pornographic intimacy. White males expressed their loathing for the sexuality they imagined black males to possess, and also their worship of it, by hideous routines of sexual torture, dismemberment, and the taking of souvenirs.

Gail Bederman has shown that black males became counterplayers in a national drama that defined white manhood during the late nineteenth century. From the time of John L. Sullivan forward white boxers frequently refused to fight blacks. When the "white hope" Jim Jeffries came out of retirement and lost to the black champion, Jack Johnson, race riots spread across the nation. Johnson's affair with a white woman triggered a massive legal vendetta: the Bureau of Investigation committed its full resources to finding some basis for a morals charge against him, obtained a conviction, and drove Johnson from the country. For whites proud of their elemental virility, Bederman argues, Johnson was a usurper of white privilege; but the manhood through which whites asserted their dominance required the projection of disowned impulses onto blacks. Johnson became not only a challenge to white manhood but an embodiment of its inner meaning.

Fantasies of primordial black sexuality play a key role in Norman Mailer's celebration of redemptive rape in *An American Dream,* where soul-destroying social routines threaten his hero's manhood. Yet Stephen Rojack, Mailer's rapist hero, confronts a spiritual menace more grievous than the "softness" that afflicted late-Victorian America amid the folkways of corporate capitalism. In the late nineteenth century the virtues of combative self-reliance could be recovered, so it seemed, by going to war, as the rhetoric of Teddy Roosevelt amply demonstrates; but early twentieth-century warfare shattered this illusion.

In *Manhood in the Making* David Gilmore observes that warrior ideals are central to the definition of manhood in many cultures because societies capable of fighting wars have generally enjoyed a selective advantage over societies that lack this capacity. The ideal asks men to risk their lives for the welfare of the society as a whole, a demand for manly self-sacrifice that has no necessary connection to individualism. But the American tradition of warrior manhood grounds its authority on exactly this connection. Warrior dignity is seen to rest on the display of individual courage, vindicating a manhood of self-command and self-reliance. Yet battlefield realities rarely, if ever, offer a fulfillment of this ideal, and the Civil War virtually refuted it. By the time Mailer wrote *An American Dream,* two world wars had raised the specter of a cosmic order, beyond the social order, in which individualist warrior virtue is meaningless. Classic

American war novels—Stephen Crane's *The Red Badge of Courage,* Ernest Hemingway's *A Farewell to Arms,* and Mailer's *The Naked and the Dead*—examine the American version of warrior manhood at war and illuminate the social realities undergirding the mythology of redemptive rape.

"The Battle Hymn of the Republic" summoned Union soldiers to redeem American society by imitating the sacrifice of Christ: "As he died to make men holy, let us die to make men free." The Gettysburg Address affirmed that the nation as a whole would realize a "new birth of freedom" because the dead men had given "the last full measure of devotion." The Revolutionary War was also an act of male procreation, Lincoln declared, in which "our fathers brought forth . . . a new nation, conceived in liberty." Men who die in battle tap the redemptive power that Harriet Beecher Stowe depicts in Uncle Tom, achieving social salvation through the shedding of their blood.

In the Civil War, young men north and south signed up for service with the confidence that soldiering was at heart the display of individual courage, Gerald Lindeman has shown, only to discover on the battlefield that heroic man-to-man encounters had little significance. At the time of the Revolution, muskets had an effective range of roughly a hundred yards; the rifled musket of the Civil War was effective at four times the distance. Defenders could now deliver multiple volleys into an advancing unit before survivors arrived at the breastwork. The result—famously at Fredericksburg and in Pickett's charge at

Gettysburg—was the slaughter of charging troops. Yet the meaning of these catastrophes was often swallowed up by the rhetoric of individual heroism. Federal leaders claimed the defeat at Fredericksburg as a spiritual triumph because wave after wave of Union soldiers had marched unflinching into the sleet of metal (Lindeman 63). Fifteen years after the war ended, General Sherman warned against such glamorous delusions in language that has been taken as a prophecy of twentieth-century warfare: "There is many a boy here today who looks on war as all glory, but, boys, it is all hell" (Royster, *Destructive* 253).

Stephen Crane's *The Red Badge of Courage* depicts Henry Fleming's quest for manhood on such a battleground. The novel does not celebrate a "new birth of freedom." Apart from occasionally designating the opposing armies as "gray" and "blue" Crane makes no indication of their political identities; and a mock-crucifixion travesties the Christian meanings of sacrificial death. Midway in his quest for manhood Henry Fleming meets a Christ figure, Jim Conklin, who has wounded hands and a wounded side and makes a strange "rite-like" progress to a seemingly preordained place of dying, attended by Fleming and a tattered man who is also badly wounded. "God," says the tattered soldier as Conklin dies—a parody of the centurion at Golgotha acknowledging the divinity of Christ. "Hell," says Henry Fleming, shaking his fist at the sky.

The "red badge" of Henry's courage is a wound he receives accidentally after he flees from his first battle. His eventual "manhood" is the reputation he obtains as he seeks to conceal this disgrace, and to counteract his shame, by fighting with headlong recklessness. Fleming's manhood is the state of being admired for wounds, forged on a battleground with no consequence beyond itself, where soldiers are primarily motivated by the terror of being shamed. Yet, on such terms, Fleming does attain manhood in battle.

Ernest Hemingway's *A Farewell To Arms* represents warfare as a holocaust of manly virtue from which his protagonist struggles to salvage his self-respect. Frederick Henry does not test himself in a great battle but is swept into a chaotic retreat after the Italian lines collapse. Warfare in this novel is not a purposeful collective enterprise but an environment in which Allied forces present as great a danger as the enemy.

Hemingway depicts a new battleground reality that redefined experience for the individual soldier. The advent of rifled muskets rendered heroic charges futile at Gettysburg and Fredericksburg; now the machine gun multiplied the firepower of the rifle fortyfold. Applied at its fullest intensity the new technology virtually abolished battle as a contest in which the soldier pits himself, and tests his courage, against threats posed by a tangible opponent.

The Somme was not the earliest World War I massacre resulting from abortive assaults, but it soon became a byword for a new and perplexing reality. The British were confident that a week of shelling would cut down the German wire and destroy their machine gun emplacements, so that the Allied troops could walk forward, occupy the German ground, and prepare for the next attack. The howitzers failed both tasks, leaving orderly rows of advancing Allied soldiers to be cut down by machine-gun fire. At the Somme this process was repeated for four and a half months and produced some 600,000 Allied casualties. Individual soldiers were "marooned," John Keegan writes, "on an undiscovered continent, where one layer of the air on which they depended for life was charged with lethal metallic particles" (*Face* 312).

Once established as the central feature of war, the new environment posed a deadly threat not only to the soldier's life but to his manhood. Rather than girding to face down a discernible enemy, out of loyalty to the community that sent him to fight, the soldier found himself disoriented and hapless on a battleground so vast and indiscriminately hostile that escape was unthinkable. Soldiers in World War I testified to

> their sense of littleness, almost of nothingness, of their
> abandonment in a physical wilderness, dominated by
> vast impersonal forces, from which even such
> normalities as the passage of time had been eliminated.
> The dimensions of the battlefield . . . extending far be-
> yond the boundaries of the individual's perception, the
> events supervening upon it—endless artillery bombard-
> ments, sudden and shatteringly powerful aerial bomb-
> ings, mass irruptions of armoured vehicles, reduced his
> subjective role, objectively vital though it was, to that of
> a mere victim. (ibid. 328)

As a form of masculine worth, the warrior ideal depends on an imaginatively compelling bond between what the soldier suffers, the cause that he serves, and the man that he is. Frederick Henry seeks to preserve the warrior manhood of individual self-respect—exemplified in legends of the American West, and in the career of Teddy Roosevelt—in a theater of war that annihilates the virtues by which that manhood is constituted. The soldier's presence amid the lethal chaos of twentieth-century war may be "objectively vital," as Keegan notes, but it despoils his manhood because it reduces to zero the value of his personal courage. Like a cow in a slaughterhouse, he has no prospect of escape and can make no meaningful vow to stand fast. Frederick Henry is haunted by the now-desecrated language. "Words such as glory, honor, courage or hallow were obscene," only an idiom of shouted speeches and "proclamations that were slapped up by billposters over other proclamations" (184–185). He "had seen nothing sacred and the things that were glorious had no glory and the sacrifices were like the stockyards at Chicago if nothing was done with the meat except bury it" (185).

Henry vindicates his masculine virtue by deserting, when he realizes that the military police will shoot him, in keeping with their mindless policy of executing officers who were separated from their regiments in the retreat. Seizing a moment when the police are distracted, Henry leaps into an icy river and makes his escape downstream. He does not renounce his warrior self-reliance but molds it into a standard of personal integrity against which he measures the warfare that has enmeshed him and finds it disgusting.

A Farewell to Arms sets the holocaust of manhood in a scenario of shameful defeat; Norman Mailer portrays it amid meaningless victory in *The Naked and the Dead.* The action takes place on a Pacific island, where U.S. Army troops confront a large Japanese force. Mailer gives center stage to Croft's platoon, which is sent on a reconnaissance mission behind the Japanese lines. The platoon stealthily circles the island by boat, cuts through the shoreline jungle, and climbs toward the summit of a mountain in the interior. Driven by Croft's savage contempt, the men pass terrifying rivers, slip past Japanese outposts, and scale impossible cliffs. But this adventure makes no contribution to the American victory, which is achieved by accident.

When General Cummings leaves the island to request naval support, his dithering subordinate orders an attack and randomly chooses a supply depot as its target. It turns out that the Japanese headquarters lies on the path toward the supply depot, so it is overrun and the main line of Japanese defense is breached; it further turns out that the Japanese have been lacking supplies for weeks. They have little ammunition and no medical equipment, and they are emaciated from lack of food. When General Cummings resumes command, nothing remains to be done but mopping up.

This concatenation of absurdities defines warfare for Mailer as the crucible of an existentialist manhood. General Cummings grasps the central reality, namely that his victory, or anyone's victory, has nothing to do with warrior virtue but is accomplished "by a random play of vulgar good luck, larded into a causal net of factors too large, too vague, for him to comprehend" (716). The blind mischances of warfare betoken cosmic absurdity, the incongruity of human purposes and dreams in a universe devoid of meaning.

But Mailer's protagonists do not discard their warrior virtues merely because those virtues are meaningless; on the contrary, they fiercely assert an individual manhood that betokens nothing beyond itself. *The Naked and the Dead* portrays warfare as a cauldron of ceaseless invidious comparison, a nightmare of competitive individualism, in which every encounter is a rivalry and the ritual of scapegoating offers men their only opportunity for communal sharing. Scapegoating in fact defines gender: victims are "women" as their triumphant victimizers momentarily become "men." Wives and girlfriends, about whom the soldiers constantly talk, are given their values by this routine. A man is always measured against other men "as either inferior or superior," General Cummings remarks. "Women play no part in it. They're an index, a yardstick among other gauges, by which to measure superiority" (322).

The popularity of *The Naked and the Dead* shows that Mailer's existentialist warrior ideal spoke to the spiritual concerns of middle-class readers in 1950s America. The power of the modern battlefield to abolish the significance of personal intention conspired with the increasing prevalence of bureaucratic organization in corporate America to generate widespread sentiments of alienation, in which the substance of personal existence seemed menaced on every side by a dehumanizing social order. The horrors of the Nazi death camps and the threat of nuclear war—the machinery of modern bureaucracy and the triumphs of modern technology placed alike in the service of mass murder—served as emblems for this nightmare.

The middle-class yearning for a primordial manhood to counteract hypercivilization now becomes sharply intensified, and Mailer takes over the fantasies of black manhood that figured in the late nineteenth-century version of this quest. In "The White Negro" Mailer celebrates the refusal to be "jailed in the prison air of other people's habits, other people's defeats, boredom, quiet desperation, and muted icy self-destroying rage" (339). To counteract this spiritual threat, Mailer recommends "the only life-giving answer," namely "to divorce oneself from society, to exist without roots ... to encourage the psychopath in oneself" (339).

Mailer's redemptive psychopath is fashioned from the lynch-mob delusions of prewar decades. He finds the model for existentialist heroism in the Negro-as-primal-orgiast. "The Negro ... could rarely afford the sophisticated inhibitions of civilization, and so he kept for his survival the arts of the primitive" (341). Blacks have been subjected to remorseless oppression in America, Mailer recognizes, but he concludes that the result has been beneficial. Bigger Thomas claims sexual violence as the keynote of his manhood, but Wright never suggests that Bigger is fortunate to have arrived at this realization. For Mailer, however, becoming a "sexual outlaw" is a spiritual fulfillment that oppressed blacks have pioneered, showing the way toward primordial manhood for whites.

Kate Millett noted the paradox that Norman Mailer is "a man whose powerful intellectual comprehension of what is most dangerous in the masculine sensibility is exceeded only by his attachment to the malaise" (314). In *An American Dream*, Mailer dramatizes the warrior manhood that rapes women in order to suppress its convulsive inner contradictions. Even as he celebrates his hero's criminal ruthlessness, Mailer anatomizes his addiction to the male-male competition that sets men against themselves and makes them most dangerous when they feel their manhood disintegrating. Women are given roles wholly subservient to this pathology; the price of resisting the hero's sexual demands is death, while women who capitulate are marvelously fulfilled.

Mailer's protagonist is Stephen Rojack, a war hero, a former U.S. Congressman, a Columbia professor, and a television personality. He is married to a rich woman whom he first met on a double date with Jack Kennedy. The manhood of Stephen Rojack is situated at the central shrines of white male prestige in America. Mailer gives the novel a vivid cast of characters: academics and socialites, policemen and mobsters; Cherry the blond nightclub singer and Shago, her black boyfriend; Rojack's wife, Deborah, and Ruta the maid. Yet Rojack's relation to these figures is derivative and trivial, even though the action is intense: he murders Deborah, rapes and sodomizes Ruta, outfaces the police, faces down the mobsters, has exultant sex with Cherry, and beats up Shago.

These tests of manhood keep Rojack gasping with anxiety, exhilarated when he prevails, but soon reeling with desperation once again. Yet these crises only prepare for the ultimate male-male showdown, his encounter with his father-in-law, Barney Kelly. Mailer tells us that Kelly "gave off the fortified good humor which is to be found in the company of generals, tycoons, politicians, admirals, newspaper publishers, and prime ministers" (219). Kelly is enormously rich, with intricate connections to an international political and economic elite. "You take all of Europe and America," Kelly remarks, "I suppose I was one of the hundred most important fellows around." His conversation with Rojack is interrupted by a phone call from President Kennedy. At issue between Rojack and Kelly is not whether Rojack has killed his daughter Deborah. Kelly already knows that and has accepted it. The point is that Kelly wants Rojack to attend Deborah's funeral so that people will recognize that the murder "has been swept under the carpet, and you and I together are in control of the situation" (233).

Deborah's death is incidental: what matters is the maintenance of male control, not only over women. If Rojack doesn't attend the funeral, Kelly fears that his male allies and antagonists will take it as a sign of weakness. The other women in the novel are likewise mere counters in the gathering confrontation of Kelly and Rojack. Rojack is startled to learn how far Kelly's power has reached into his own crises. Via the FBI and the White House, Kelly arranged for Rojack to be released by the police; and he did this for the same reason that he planted Ruta in Deborah's household as a spy. Deborah's elaborate love life, which brought on the rage in which Rojack killed her, was only incidentally meant to insult Rojack. The real target was Kelly, her father. Deborah took spies for lovers—men under surveillance by the CIA—so that Kelly (and President Kennedy) would worry that her pillow-talk was giving away political secrets.

Deborah's motive for tormenting her father was revenge for in-
cest, a program of sexual exploitation Kelly had initiated when
she was fifteen. Ruta, also sexual provender for Kelly, hopes to
use her knowledge of Deborah's affairs to blackmail Kelly into
marrying her. Cherry too has been Kelly's mistress, Rojack
learns, by way of his gangland connections.

When he enters Kelly's inner sanctum of male power, Rojack
arrives at the source of his sexual longings. An erotic fusion
takes place between the men that is cemented by their having
partaken of the same three women. Like fraternity boys at a
gang rape, the men connect with each other sexually through
the women. But the reverse is equally true; the men connect
with women sexually by way of their relationships with one another. Not only is male desire for women absorbed into the intimate rivalry of men with men; the passions of that male-male
wrestling give structure to the desire that draws them to
women. What counts as heterosexual desire in Rojack is a pattern of impulses governed by the effort to assert his manhood
in competition with other men and by his need to overcome the
contradictions that threaten to collapse that manhood from
within. Mailer elaborates the union between male-male contest
and male-female sex and seals it through a sustained allusion to
Rojack's rectal intercourse with Ruta. Kelly's "body gave off the
radiation of a fire, there was heat between us now the way there
had been heat between Ruta and me . . . Suddenly I knew what it
had been like with Cherry and him, not so far from Ruta and
me, no, not so far and I knew what it had been like with

Deborah and him, what a hot burning two-backed beast . . . 'Come on,' Kelly murmured, sitting on his throne, 'shall we get shitty?'" (254).

Rojack's penis digs into the feces in Ruta's rectum when he sodomizes her, and what he calls "the canny hard-packed evil in that butt" becomes an emblem for the complex and impacted layers of male power that he penetrates—from Deborah to Ruta to Cherry—in coming face to face with Kelly. Rojack's homophobic male-male intercourse with Kelly is symbolically foretold when he murders Deborah, rapes Ruta, and takes possession of Cherry; and he derives from this procession of triumphs the inner empowerment that he needs to face Kelly down. Despite the massive prestige and dark power Kelly brings to his threats and blandishments, Rojack refuses to bend to his will: he simply won't go to the funeral.

Rojack's effort to vindicate his manhood in *An American Dream* triumphs in this amazingly silly moment; it begins in rape and sexual murder. Rojack embodies a riven manhood sick with desire. Besieged by inner panic, he chronically disowns his helplessness and vulnerability by projecting it onto women. The women in Rojack's life live on a knife-edge. When they shield him from his inner terrors he adores them. When they challenge him and intensify those terrors, his adoration turns into murderous fury.

Rojack is humiliated by the awareness that his wife's money and family connections have sponsored his political career. This enrages him because it reveals "how unconsummated and unmasculine was the core of my force" (18). Rojack believes he should be completely self-commanding, and his marriage to Deborah "was the armature of my ego; remove the armature and I might topple like clay" (17). When Deborah tells him she's finished with him, Rojack loses his grip. "I did not belong to myself any longer. Deborah had occupied my center . . . In another minute I would begin to grovel" (27).

Deborah's murder only peripherally involves Deborah: it is an experience Rojack has with Rojack, and the unfolding of his inner awareness takes center stage. His fury feels portentous, far in excess of her insults; as he strangles her, he pushes open a doorway to paradise; when her neck cracks and she stops twitching, he floats blissfully into a new world of masculine fulfillment. "I opened my eyes. I was weary with most honorable fatigue, and my flesh seemed new" (32). "Deborah's dying," he later observes, "had given me a new life" (93).

Murder is orgasm for Rojack, and orgasm is murder: both are moments when a man enhances and confirms his manhood by bending another to his will. In Deborah he conquers a woman who resists this program; the opposing scenario is enacted immediately thereafter when he rapes Ruta. Ruta objects when Rojack works his penis into her rectum, and he obligingly transfers it to her vagina. But then he stakes his sovereign claim: "I jammed up her ass and came as if I'd been flung across the room" (46), to the tune of Ruta's cries of pain and rage. Ruta's subjugation is essential to Rojack's fulfillment, but it is equally essential—so Mailer affirms—to Ruta's fulfillment. "I do not know why you have trouble with your wife," she tells him. "You are absolutely a genius, Mr. Rojack" (46).

This encounter gives Rojack nerve enough to go back upstairs and throw his wife's body out the window, but not
enough to surmount the terrors aroused by his dealings with
the police. The emotional support needed for that task is provided by Cherry, who catches his eye as the detectives are examining Deborah's body on the pavement. Rojack quickly establishes a mystical infatuation with Cherry in which she becomes
yet another talisman of his manhood. She "belongs" to Italian
gangsters—including Romeo, a prizefighter—who gather at the
nightclub where she sings. At the nightclub Rojack becomes
obsessed with Cherry's "money-counter, Southern-girl ass," an
emblem of the male hierarchy of potency and money and of
Rojack's sorry place in it. "'This bee-hind is for sale, boy,' it said
to me, 'but you ain't got the price'" (97).

As Rojack gets drunker and drunker, he is enveloped by anxiety: "A sickness came off her, something broken and dead . . . It
drifted in a pestilence of mood toward my table, sickened me as
it settled in" (100). Rojack suffers the endemic inner sickness of
self-sufficient valorous men, and becomes their expiation and
apotheosis when he staggers to the bathroom and throws up.
For Mailer, this attainment of sainthood possesses the utmost
solemnity:

> The rot and gas of compromise, the stink of old fears,
> mildew of discipline, all the biles of habit and the hor-
> rors of pretence—ah, here was the heart of the puke—
> came thundering out . . . I felt like some gathering
> wind, which drew sickness from the lungs and livers of

> others and passed them through me and up and out
> into the water . . . If the murderer were now loose in me,
> well, so too was a saint of sorts, a minor saint, no
> doubt, but free at last to absorb the ills of others and
> regurgitate them forth . . . I washed my face in cold wa-
> ter, but carefully . . . as if I were washing a new face.
> (101)

The face of his renewed manhood firmly in place, Rojack now has little difficulty staring down Romeo and the other gangsters. He takes Cherry to her apartment for a series of apocalyptic orgasms and defeats Shago when he shows up with his knife.

Deborah, Ruta, and Cherry are figures of an imagination that invests women's bodies with meanings drawn from the requirements of manhood. Yet Mailer's anatomy of such manhood can serve a purpose Mailer did not contemplate, that of repudiating this masculinity as intrinsically pathological and seeking more just and humane alternatives.

An American Dream, as Mailer dreams it—shared by no matter how many American men and enshrined in no matter how eloquent a literary tradition—is an American nightmare. Like racist notions that deal out systematic injustice to blacks, Mailer's manhood is fundamentally hostile to the requirements of justice in a democracy. As women assert full citizenship, and find their own voices, men must dismantle the tradition of male gendering that presupposes female inferiority. Mailer proposes that the abuse of women is an exercise in manly courage, heroically sustaining itself in the desperate and vertiginous solitary struggle against other men. But the truth is entirely the reverse: the manhood Mailer celebrates is cowardice.

For men to shrink from facing the miseries inherent to their lives is not brave; nor is it brave for men to evade that confrontation by imagining womanhoods in which masculine dilemmas can be concealed, whether a Gorgon like Deborah, a glutton for abuse like Ruta, or a trophy like Cherry. Using women to bolster male egos violates women's right to define their own lives, and one might conclude by saying it is also a chickenshit way for men to live. But denunciation alone will not avail for men whose selves are deformed by this tradition of manhood, any more than long-suffering feminine sympathy and forgiveness avail. Courage cannot be mustered effectively to face the liabilities inherent to this way of being manly, so long as the act of mustering courage itself unconsciously reenacts the drama of manhood conquering womanly weakness. Yet courage worthy of the name has always required the willingness to face one's own patterns of self-defeat. The effort to cultivate and honor democratic masculinities must surmount the paradoxes of misogynist braggadocio by realizing a wholly different drama, in which the war of the sexes is not incorporated into the definition of manhood, but women and men engage each other on grounds of equality and mutual respect.

7

Democratic Masculinities

A T THE SECOND Continental Congress in 1776, John Adams received a letter from his wife Abigail asking him to support laws that would strip "vicious" men of their power to treat women with "cruelty and indignity." "Do not put such unlimited power into the hands of the Husbands," she requested (121). Amid the multitude of legal and political disabilities that Abigail Adams suffered as an American woman in the late eighteenth century, she singles out domestic abuse—including sexual abuse—for special emphasis. The charter of citizen equality that John Adams was building at the Convention would eventually be taken as a warrant for enlarging the protections and powers guaranteed to women by law. But the bed-and-board issues on which Abigail demanded action from the outset still constitute a harshly contested frontier. John Adams himself responded to Abigail's concerns with derision. "As to your extraordinary code of laws," he wrote back, "I cannot but laugh" (122).

From Adams's time forward, men have opposed women seeking to establish their rights. The Seneca Falls Convention of 1848, the nineteenth-century effort to assert the property rights of married women, the suffrage fight that ended in 1920, and the quest for equal economic opportunity and sexual autonomy that commenced in the 1960s: all these have surmounted various forms of male resistance. The gains of women have at times motivated reactionary social movements led by men, as in the "rough rider" vogue of the late nineteenth century and the current resurgence of male dominance on the agenda of the religious right. The defeat of the Equal Rights Amendment in 1982, narrow as it was, gave renewed confidence to the contemporary defenders of male privilege.

A countercurrent runs through this story of feminist advance and male resistance, however, men supporting the cause of equality for women, sometimes as the spouses of feminist leaders. When he married Angelina Grimké in 1838, Theodore Dwight Weld refused his legal rights. According to Angelina's sister Sarah, the two "abjured all authority, all government, save the influence which love would give them over each other as moral and immortal beings" (Abzug 226). William Lloyd Garrison agreed with the Grimké sisters that the cause of women's rights should be coupled with the movement to abolish slavery, even though many abolitionists (including Weld) thought it unadvisable. "I have been derisively called a 'Woman's Rights Man,' Garrison proclaimed: "I know of no such distinction. I claim to be a HUMAN RIGHTS MAN, and wherever there is human being, I see God-given rights inherent in that being, whatever may be the sex or complexion" (Sellers 407). William Sanger supported his wife Margaret's work on behalf of birth control, and when the agents of Anthony Comstock put him on trial in 1915, he took the occasion to declare himself: "I am proud to be identified with the work of that noble woman, Margaret Sanger," he told the court (Kimmel and Mosmiller 351).

In our own time, Pepper Schwartz has observed, men who seek egalitarian marriages are generally not ideologues, to say nothing of being prominent figures. Many in the historical record of male support for feminist causes were men of very modest renown. In 1825 the otherwise unknown William Thompson published a work protesting the "civil and domestic slavery" of women; Michael Kimmel and Thomas Mosmiller have uncovered the likewise obscure profeminist writings of Mathew Carey (1830), Jonathan Neal (1843), the Rev. L. Clark Seelye (1874), William L. Bowditch (1885), Pradexis Guerrero (1910), and Floyd Dell (1917).

Men supporting women's efforts have braved public humiliation and ridicule. William Sanger was convicted on charges of distributing "obscene, lewd, lascivious, filthy, indecent and disgusting" literature, hardly a laughing matter at the time (ibid. 351). Defenders of masculine privilege in the late nineteenth century created a new vocabulary of abuse. Male reformers "sing falsetto," declared Senator John Ingalls of Kansas in 1886: they are "effeminate without being either masculine or feminine . . . possessing neither fecundity or virility: endowed with the contempt of men and the derision of women." A man befriending feminist causes was a "prudish Miss Nancy," a "sissy" of puny and enfeebled physique, with "small hands, small feet, a receding chin, and a culture much above his intellect" (Rotundo 272). The courage to face derision has been asked of men endorsing feminist projects, as of men supporting any embattled cause.

But a special brand of courage is required when external ridicule is echoed within the masculine self. Code manhood is enforced in large measure through unconscious practices of self-derision, which are activated by the prospect of disloyalty to the code. Tim O'Brien describes his defeat by these internal/external voices when he contemplated refusing to serve in Vietnam: "In my head I could hear people screaming at me. Traitor! They yelled. Turncoat! Pussy! I felt myself blush. I couldn't tolerate it. I couldn't endure the mockery... and right then I submitted. I would go to the war . . . because I was embarrassed not to" (Things 61–62). He became a soldier because he shrank from the battle that would follow if he refused: "I was a coward, I went to the war" (63).

Students of the fitfully active "men's movement" have pointed out that men lack grievances to organize around. Men committed to gender justice plumb their inner lives in vain to find resentments arising from male dominance that merit political redress. The absence of sustained collective male opposition to the sexual abuse of women finds an explanation here: the vexations of men that give rise to violence against women do not result from causes that allow men to unite *as men* against a common enemy.

On the bed-and-board frontier, in particular, men are inhibited by sexual responses we have been trained to consider inseparable from maleness. John Stoltenberg proposes that men renounce "manhood"; he declares that finding egalitarian intimacy with women depends on "refusing to be a man." Stoltenberg is right to imply that efforts to reconstruct "manhood" as a new monolith, against which all men must judge themselves, are doomed to failure, since that would only reformulate the grounds for perpetuating an invidious anti-womanhood. But men who seek gender justice will continue to be men, and should be encouraged to develop masculinities that variously incorporate biological maleness, even as they repudiate the legacy of patriarchal oppression and respond to the initiatives and demands brought by those directly injured.

Cultivating democratic masculinities entails a twofold struggle. Men must work to prohibit practices that violate women's sexual autonomy, and they must also work to confront their own chronic anxieties directly. Rather than using women to conceal and allay them, men must track their anxieties to their true sources in the dilemmas of code manhood and in the social injustices this version of masculinity helps to conceal.

Such a paradoxical enterprise, fusing judgment and prohibition with compassionate understanding, lies at the heart of a sex offenders' therapy program in Austin, Texas, led by Dr. Deanna Garza-Louis and Dr. Fred Dooley, whose weekly sessions they allowed me to attend. The group includes men whose lives have been marked by public masturbation, wife beating, and child molestation. Most are in therapy as a condition of parole. Dr. Garza-Louis notes that a prison term of one to three months suffices to cancel the tacit permission men are given to engage in coercive sexual behavior, but is short enough to forestall socialization into the abusive prison culture. Blue collar and white collar, Tejano and Anglo, well educated and high-school dropouts, intensely pious and completely unchurched, these men share the task of halting their sexual misconduct and rebuilding their lives on new grounds. Dr. Dooley defines the goal of treatment as "Better Than Well," meaning an existence that transcends the pathologies that mar the lives of "normal" men. In order to gain control over their addiction to sexual offenses, they must obtain a capacity for honest intimacy sorely needed by men whose destructive conduct is legal.

This requires surmounting the double bind built into code manhood, according to which self-condemnation itself produces compulsive behavior. The programs of therapy for "nonrelational sexuality" developed by Ronald Levant and William Pollack resist any hint of feminist "male-bashing" because of the recognition that moral indictment by itself rarely empowers an offender to change his conduct. When a self-despising program of self-control leads a man to project his despised unmanly impulses onto a woman or a child, then "just say no" sooner or later yields a sickening "yes," and new offenses follow. But despite their nonjudgmental air, the new therapy programs depend at least tacitly on the threat of real sanctions. Economically competent women are equipped to ensure that men who refuse to confront their sexual problems will lose their wives (or partners) and children.[1]

Men commit injustices that must stop; they do severe injuries to real victims. The effort to avoid the destructive consequences of "male bashing" must not yield an approach aimed wholly at cultivating self-awareness. Focusing exclusively on the emotional skills that men need to gain, without enforcing the legal protections their victims deserve or teaching the behavioral and cognitive practices that enable them to halt their destructive conduct, will only produce what Roger Wolfe calls "sex offenders with insight" (Salter 130). Sessions accordingly work back and forth between poles that at first seem incompatible—asserting (and enforcing) legal and moral prohibitions while encouraging the men to look upon their crippled psyches with understanding and compassion.

Conversations focus on seasons of liability, "high-risk" occasions when pornographic impulses grow intense. The anxieties prompting such impulses arise from a multitude of personal circumstances, typically introduced as insignificant. "I was having a tough time back then," said Archer about accosting his girlfriend's thirteen-year-old daughter when she stepped out of the shower, pushing her against the wall, and touching her breasts and genitals.

Here is a translation of "a tough time" as it emerged over several weeks. Archer is a highly conscientious man, the son of a Baptist minister who was by turns remote and harshly intrusive. Archer for years remained a faithful churchman. He is a skilled finish carpenter, capable of taking responsibility for complicated projects and completing them without supervision. Things seemed to be going well, but then his wife divorced him, in his view unaccountably. She gained custody of their two children. He began to drink heavily and to frequent topless bars, met a drug-addicted dancer, and took her home to his apartment, hoping to rescue her from her wretched life, a project that soon failed. He then moved in with a woman named Tiffany. Archer's work deteriorated: he started using tricks to make his jobs look better than they were. As his pride in his craftsmanship disappeared, he came to feel that his job was nothing but slavery. After being criticized for bad performance, he took a job with a builder who did huge residential subdivisions and wasn't alert to sloppy work. From this employer Archer soon began to steal small sums of money. When Tiffany told him she was pregnant, Archer declared he would marry her; she replied that another man was the father; he believed this was a lie, concocted because she wanted to abort the child without opposition from him, as she proceeded to do. Then came Archer's assault on Tiffany's daughter.

This chronicle—powerless shame and confusion, dissolving competence, drunkenness, sexual degradation, a life miserably and inexplicably out of control—he at times recounted as a madcap adventure:

> I was in the toilet, man. One woman takes my babies,
> and another woman kills one, and not a thing I could
> do about it. And me drunk all the time, on the money I
> was stealing from my sorry-ass employer, and me doing
> sorry-ass work, and wondering where my children were

at, and my ex wouldn't even talk to me on the phone, and hanging out in porno shops and titty bars, and feeling up this kid. I had turned into a creep, man. I'm glad I got busted. Something had to turn my life around.

"That's a lot of crap," replied another group member. "This isn't any upbeat deal, and getting busted won't turn you around. What are you bragging about? It's a world of hurt here."

What followed was a long silence, Archer staring into space. "I had a dream last night," he finally said. "I had my two babies in my arms, and they were both skinny, with bloated bellies, like those famine victims on TV. They were crying and crying, wanting something to eat, and twisting and thrashing in my arms. I had nothing to give them. No food for them. No comfort. I just had to stand there hearing them."

Silence continued for several moments, and then the men offered interpretations: the dream is about Archer missing his children, about knowing they need nourishment he can't give them, about his helplessness in the face of their need. And/or the dream is about Archer's own deep-lying emotional starvation and agony, arising from his abusive relation to his own father. And/or the dream is about Archer becoming able to recognize his own helplessness and inner pain, able to take it into his arms.

Producing such moments of searching awareness is only one aspect of the process, and hard questions remain about Archer's story. Did Tiffany abort his child because it was con-

ceived in a rape? Did his effort to "rescue" the topless dancer include supplying her with drugs to keep her dependent on him?
The abusive control exercised in the criminal assault clearly had
precursors, quite possibly in the marriage that Archer's wife
had found intolerable.

Such explorations contribute to undoing the enchantment
that holds men fast, insofar as abusive sexuality conceals and
allays inner desperation. When Archer joined the group, his sexual offense was "just a really stupid thing to do." He saw no
connection to the chaos that had taken over his life or to the
torment in his relationship with his father. Nor did he recognize his ebullience as a cover for shame and confusion. The
other men in the group, who have trouble seeing their own eva-
sive patterns, quickly recognized Archer's and saw how his sexual misconduct worked as a narcotic. Acquiring inner awareness will not remove the social, economic, and educational
disadvantages that contribute to Archer's anxieties, which are
now compounded by his legal problems. But learning to see
through his pornographic sensibility to the hard realities it
conceals puts Archer in a new position, from which he can de-
ploy his intelligence and courage against true sources of his sexually violent impulses.

I distinctly recall the first instant I saw these men, lounging
and smoking on the steps of the counseling center. They composed an image of child molesters as moral monsters. I saw
them as beings wholly alien to myself, but before the first ses-
sion ended, I recognized that their discussions focused on the
very issues of manhood I'd been exploring, and possessed a de-

gree of candor and insight I had never before encountered. Far from standing at the margins of conventional manhood, these men are working at its troubled center. And the microculture of this group sustains and reflects pressures that are generated by political and economic changes going forward in contemporary American society at large.

When the Texas economy failed in the mid 1980s there appeared a bumper sticker—"Shit Happens"—that summed up the catastrophe for blue-collar workers like Archer, who did not understand the classic economic logic of cartels, which led to the failure of OPEC, producing the collapse of the Texas oil business and the construction industry, which crashed the banks. Male anxieties are often spurred by the local impact of broad historical developments that may hardly be visible to the man in question, much less intelligible. Still, "Shit Happens" is better than the sexist response, which allays shaken masculine competence through fantasies of dominating women. Sexism works like racism; it blinds sexists to the sources of their oppression.

Despotic manhood conveys a delusory sensation of majestic privilege, the domination of women and of "feminine" men concealing the reality of male disempowerment. As Joseph Pleck observes, the fantasies of self-determination that are bolstered by sexism prompt men to hold themselves individually answerable for their own calamities, reading as "personal failure" the outcome of conditions beyond their control ("Men's Power" 413–420). "Shit Happens," while inadequate as analysis, at least recognizes that the blue-collar worker who loses his job needs to look beyond himself to find the reason.

As the twenty-first century dawns, relatively privileged white men, who once enjoyed secure managerial and technical positions in major U.S. corporations, find themselves similarly under threat. The mutual loyalty that once obtained between them and their employers has collapsed, so that very well compensated workers no longer expect to stay with the same company for any extended period. Like migrant laborers in the fields, they are subject to fluctuating opportunities that are generated and canceled by distant and mysterious economic processes. The ultimate economy is no longer the national economy but a transnational corporate order that has outflanked organized labor, has reduced access to the middle class, and is now bringing national governments under its discipline. The command centers of this new order are information centers, detached from local cultures by the character of the cyberspace networks through which information passes. At the top of the new hierarchy is a super-rich class, featuring celebrities like Bill Gates and Ted Turner, while members of local elites and their middle-class employees lose control of their destinies. This disempowerment of formerly solid citizens, taking place as the blue-collar labor of many Americans becomes superfluous, recalls the late nineteenth-century pattern and has bred a fanatical cult of self-sufficient manhood.

Through the "Promise Keepers," and in countless local settings, the religious right seeks to rehabilitate a morality in which individual self-discipline and male dominance within the family will suffice to recapture the vanished social empowerment. As in the late nineteenth century, this reactionary impulse has also produced unprecedented adulation for national sports heroes and a remarkably increased tolerance for violence in the arena. Gorgeous George with his golden curls, the most famous professional wrestler of the 1950s, has given way to The Monster, The Undertaker, and Stone Cold Steve Austin. Who can remember when the word "vicious"—applied to a football player—was intended as a criticism?

William Nack and Lester Munson describe the rising cost to the men who play professional football in a *Sports Illustrated* article entitled "The Wrecking Yard." Nack and Munson report that the number of players suffering a major injury—requiring surgery or forcing the player to miss eight games or more—increased from 42 percent before 1959 to 72 percent in the 1980s. Degenerative arthritis—resulting from the abuse dealt out to cartilage in knees, hips, and back—produces lifelong impairment, as does the harm created by drugs that allow injured players to continue playing. The paralysis now afflicting Johnny Unitas's right hand (from which such miracles flew forth) is not an aberrant misfortune, but speaks for "a whole society of broken men hounded through their lives by pain and injury, and all the psychological problems that often attend them" (65). Yet the public appetite for such mayhem remains overpowering, and young men eagerly sacrifice their bodies to satisfy it. The movie *Gladiator* made the point that collective bloodlust overcame the Roman populace as democratic institutions deteriorated, but the film did not check the corresponding American mania. What captured attention were the spectacular scenes of killing.

The heroics of gladiatorial decadence also appear in the rhetoric that proponents of this cultural movement direct against their political antagonists: "Liberalism is an essentially feminine, submissive worldview," declares a champion of the new male triumphalism. "It is the worldview of men who do not have the moral toughness, and spiritual strength to stand up and do single combat with life" (Macdonald). The masculinist self-hatred at work in this woman-hating rhetoric also sustains the booming porn industry, even as ideologues of the religious right decry it. That Larry Flynt and Jerry Falwell are engaged in the same cultural work—that of bolstering self-sufficient manhood—is nicely emblematized in the careers of Jimmy Swaggart and Jim Bakker, whose abusive sexual escapades both echoed and disrupted their sexy careers as televangelists. As in the moral crusades of the early nineteenth century, it remains true today that porn and the denunciation of porn blur into each other; a hip upscale instance of this fusion is *American Psycho,* in which a parade of hideous sexual murders excites both horror and pleasure.

We inhabit today a sharply polarized culture: the movement toward gender justice remains vital, even amid resurgent male supremacy. The debates that followed the war in Vietnam included clamorous efforts to reclaim the lost masculine honor on traditional terms, as in the "standing tall" rhetoric broadcast during the actions in Grenada, Nicaragua, and Iraq. But there has also been a powerful current of reassessment. A grass-roots movement of Vietnam veterans devoted itself to healing the psychic traumas inflicted by the war, men showing the courage to face those traumas and to explore their sources. What in earlier wars was contemptuously dismissed as "shell shock" is now understood as post-traumatic stress disorder, with the clear recognition that nothing shameful happens when a man is psychologically overwhelmed. Maya Lin's Vietnam Memorial became a national shrine for the validation of unashamed masculine grieving.

After President Nixon ended the draft, it soon became apparent that adequate military forces could not be maintained by means of the available men, and that women attracted to the military were on average better educated and more reliable than men. Linda Bird Francke, in *Ground Zero: The Gender Wars in the Military*, chronicles the abuse dealt out to women making their way into military careers, where they threaten "men's real or imagined sense of virility" (156). Francke details a luxuriant culture of pornography and topless dancers, gratuitous leg-spreader exercises, and impromptu sexual assaults, as well as rape and harassment in training camps, in officers clubs, and in the military academies.

Defenders of this tradition affirm that American fighting men cannot function without the consolation available through sexual abuse, nor can they tolerate the presence of women who are unsuited for such abuse, that is, competent women warriors. Defending the sexual offenses committed at the 1991 Tailhook convention, Jerry R. Cadick, USMC Ret., pines for the days before "the Navy's wake-up call to 'political correctness,'" when "we got together and behaved like the barbarians that our profession demanded of us." Violent misogyny must be instilled in fighting men, George Gilder explains: "If you want to create a solidaristic group of male killers, you kill the woman in them" (Francke 155). In a 1992 Presidential Commission report, Major C. B. Johnson summed it up: "the warrior mentality will crumble if women are placed in combat positions" (ibid. 260).

Flogging was defended in the nineteenth-century U.S. navy on notably similar arguments: its champions maintained that discipline would collapse if the captain were forbidden to have sailors lashed. As in the slaveholding South, the purpose of flogging on shipboard was to maintain a hierarchy of persons deemed unequal, just as males and females are deemed unequal in the mentality of despotic manhood. Flogging was a device through which subordinates were "broken," to instill a disposition in keeping with their place, a function likewise served by rape and wife beating. In the 1830s and 1840s flogging at school and in the household became topics of fierce debate, as the requirements of democratic equality were applied to male laborers and were extended more tentatively to women and children. The naval establishment of that era was caught in the transition; some officers viewed themselves, like slaveholders, as "gentlemen" exercising aristocratic authority over the "common seamen." Herman Melville spoke for the emerging majority in 1850 when he denounced the practice as "utterly repugnant to the spirit of our democratic institutions" (146). Flogging was soon outlawed with no discernible harm to national security.

The schooling of officers at West Point is currently being reformed in response to the presence of woman cadets. As Michael Winerip notes, it is a new form of the long-standing challenge: "How to produce warrior-officers vicious enough to kill and sensitive enough to inspire the troops of a democratic nation to follow" (48). The leadership at West Point has determined that discipline and mental toughness can be instilled without the sexualized humiliation of men and without assaults on women. This entails confronting attitudes many male cadets bring with them. An educational program opposing sexual harassment begins when the cadets arrive, and the school takes prompt disciplinary action when cases are reported.

Conservative alumni are uneasy about these reforms. "I keep hearing we're destroying the soul of the warrior," says General Daniel W. Christman, West Point's superintendent. But the training regimen remains demanding, and records on physical fitness reveal that the women in the class of 1997 are in better shape than were the men of 1962. Women cadets still confront sexual jokes and demeaning comments, and the aim of constructing a new model of military character is far from fulfillment. Yet the project has potentially far-reaching implications.

Women in the armed forces may pioneer new ways to cultivate a warrior temperament, not steeling themselves for combat by despising "cunts" and "pussies" or allaying their anxiety through fantasies of raping women. The gender-integrated military may also provide a setting in which men will fashion new manhoods. Young men in the regular army today sometimes find themselves confronted in boot camp with a female drill sergeant, who presents herself and her harsh demands as a model of the warrior character that the recruit is expected to form in himself.

The virtues of tenderness and compassion traditionally defined as "feminine" are real virtues, and many women fear they will be discarded if women become "male identified" in military careers. Perhaps as a consequence, women Vietnam veterans have been notably absent from the leadership of the women's movement, and the problems of women in the military have received only belated attention from feminists (Bates 168). Yet social order itself, civil or international, can only be maintained so long as it is policed, which means that the disciplined use of deadly force remains a social necessity, and there is no reason males should retain a monopoly on it. Military life has long provided access to social advantage for marginalized groups, most recently for African Americans; and women may likewise find a path to public leadership through the armed forces. Should that happen, it will diminish the fraudulent authority accruing to despotic manhood from its association with military service.

Powerful works of contemporary literature portray misogynist violence as a misfortune of socialization, not a primordial endowment. Russell Banks's *Affliction* acknowledges the long-standing traditions that sustain code manhood but treats them as traditions, not as facts of nature, and suggests new possibilities.

Banks's protagonist, Wade Whitehouse, clings forlornly to a vision of his own humanity, which he projected onto his high school sweetheart, Lillian, and sought to maintain by marrying her. Wade bears a legacy of boyhood brutalization, dealt out by a wife-beating father who relentlessly humiliated his sons in the effort to make "men" of them. But Wade is unconscious of his inner distress; Banks likens his soul to a frozen pond on which a solid sheet of ice separates the world above from what lies beneath. Seeking to repudiate his father's violence, Wade finds himself hopelessly ensnared, because headlong rage overwhelms him when the pain surfaces. Wade is dangerous to those who care most for him; he beats his wife and his subsequent girlfriend, and he cultivates paranoid delusions that lead him to murder a friend and co-worker as well as his father.

Banks offers Wade's fate as an exceptionally bloody version of the tragedy that afflicts an enduring tradition of manhood:

> the lives of boys and men for thousands of years, boys
> beaten by their fathers, whose capacity for love and
> trust was crippled almost at birth and whose best hope
> for a connection to other human beings lay in elaborat-
> ing for themselves an elegiac mode of relatedness, as if
> everyone's life were already over. It is how we keep from
> destroying in our turn our own children and terroriz-
> ing the women who have the misfortune to love us; it is

how we absent ourselves from the tradition of male violence; it is how we decline the seductive role of avenging
angel: we grimly accept the restraints of nothingness—
of disconnection, isolation and exile. (340)

Hypermasculine hysteria like that of Wade Whitehouse is
played for black comedy in *Fargo*, the Oscar-winning film written by Joel and Ethan Coen. Jerry Lundegaard devises a cruel
and crackpot scheme to have his wife kidnapped so as to extort
ransom from his hated rich father-in-law, who insists on confronting the kidnappers with a pistol and dies in the shootout.
The kidnappers are likewise addicted to invidious male-male
competition. Carl Showalter is an obscene loudmouth who
seizes every occasion for spiteful quarreling, while his partner
Gayle Grimsrud is a strong silent type, a Marlboro man addicted to Marlboro cigarettes. As this quartet of vicious clowns
play out their farce of kidnapping and murder, Marge Gunderson tracks them down. A pregnant police chief, Gunderson is not a "man," nor is she the opposite of a man. Unlike the
stereotypical hard-eyed detective, she does not commune
with the dark secrets of the criminal heart. "I just don't get
it," she says as she drives Grimsrud off to jail, "and such a nice
day, too. And for nothing but a little money." Yet Marge
is a consummate investigator; decisive, persistent, smart, and
brave.

The confrontation between Gunderson and Grimsrud portrays the delirious excess of violence to which the males are

prone, as opposed to her commonsense use of force. She finds Grimsrud in the act of running Carl's body through a wood-chipper, which produces a spray of gore from the exit chute. In the entrance chute is what remains of Carl's leg, the foot stubbornly resisting Grimsrud's frantic effort to jam it into the machinery. Squinting down the barrel of her pistol, Gunderson shouts for Grimsrud to surrender, and when he hesitates she points to the badge on her cap. The contrast with the classic male-male confrontation could not be clearer: instead of a fist-fight demonstrating who is the better "man," we have a confrontation between a "man" and the law, of which Marge is the agent. When Grimsrud runs away, she shoots once and misses. Then she hits him in the back of the leg. Her use of force is not supernaturally skillful, as is the norm when a John Wayne hero pulls the trigger; but it gets the job done.

In *Affliction* and *Fargo* male pathologies take center stage, but standing at the edge of each narrative is a male figure that suggests the possibility of a better manhood. Rolfe Whitehouse tells his brother's story with unsparing clarity, seeing Wade's stunted capacity for love as well as his cruelty. The brothers were bred to the same affliction, Rolfe tells us, chips off the same old block; they have remained close, even as Rolfe has disengaged himself from the male culture that holds Wade captive. When he was young, Rolfe was like Wade, "troublesome, violent, male. Later, with excruciating difficulty, he would change, but no one in the family knew that, except possibly Wade" (95). Banks doesn't tell us Rolfe's story, though we do learn that he is unmarried, childless, and alone. "Disconnection, isolation and exile" may have freed Rolfe from the tradition of male violence, but the life he now leads is bleak.

Norm Gunderson occupies a comparably marginal narrative position in *Fargo;* we meet him in bed with Marge, when she takes the early-morning phone call that reports the first murder, and he insists on making her breakfast. Norm appears in five short scenes that punctuate the fast-paced thriller with moments of quiet, when he and Marge have lunch or curl up in bed together. Norm is a painter and has entered his painting of a mallard duck in a contest sponsored by the Post Office. As the two settle down to sleep at the film's end, Norm tells Marge mournfully that his mallard failed to take first place and will appear only on three-cent stamps. "No," Marge remonstrates, "It's terrific." She points out that his stamp will be used a lot, because people need the little stamps when the cost of postage changes. "It's terrific," she insists: "I'm so proud of you."

Apart from his interest in fishing, that's all we learn about Norm Gunderson. We see him at bed and board with Marge, as the two look forward to the birth of their child; and his gentleness and solicitude form a telling counterpoint to the hysterical competitiveness, self-alienation, and sexual cruelty of the leading male figures. In fact he establishes the moral center, the "norm," that anchors the Coens' depiction of hypermasculine delirium. Yet while he dramatizes the possibility of a fertile, competent, and intimate manhood, we do not see that manhood under construction. Norm has no need, it seems, to struggle against the inner demons that possess other men.

Pat Conroy's *The Prince of Tides* recounts such a struggle. It tells the story of Tom Wingo, overtaken in his mid-thirties by three disasters: his brother is killed, his sister attempts suicide, and his wife tells him she's having an affair. Wingo is a high school football coach leading an apparently stable and happy life; his wife, Sallie, is a successful physician. He shares fully in housekeeping and childcare and has become a gourmet cook. Yet he carries a hidden legacy of torment.

Tom's early life dramatizes the parallel victimization of women and growing boys at the hands of violent men. Wingo's father was a wife-beater who whipped his sons in the effort to make them "men"; and when a trio of criminals assault his mother, they also rape Tom. As he comes to maturity, Tom repudiates his father's teaching: "I learned everything there was to know about being a man from you, Dad," he declares. "I learned that it's normal for a man to beat his wife. I learned that its normal for a man to beat his children" (577).

His wife's affair blows apart Wingo's humane and tranquil life, compelling him to reckon with the emotional detachment that had made their marriage unbearable for her. "I thought I had succeeded in not becoming a violent man, but . . . my violence was subterranean, unbeheld. It was my silence, my long withdrawals, that I had turned into dangerous things . . . I had figured out how to live a perfectly meaningless life, but one that could . . . destroy the lives of those around me" (101).

Wingo's struggle with his schooling in violent masculinity unfolds in relation to paired alter egos, equally victims of the family's crippling legacy. His sister Savannah is a gifted and successful poet, living in New York, who suffers psychotic episodes in which she turns her rage against herself. His brother Luke is a Navy Seal who embraces heroic violence and dies pursuing a solo terrorist campaign against corporate interests that seek to build a nuclear power plant in the tidal marshland where the Wingo siblings grew up.

Tom travels from his native South Carolina to New York City in order to care for his sister and undertakes an effort to break free of the dichotomy that separates these "feminine" and "masculine" responses to the core trauma. As he waits in her outer office to meet Dr. Susan Lowenstein, Savannah's therapist, Wingo recognizes his underlying dilemma, the double bind that permits him to be manly and competent only on terms that destroy his emotional vitality:

> It was good to feel the tears try to break through. It was proof I was still alive inside, down deep, where the hurt lay bound and degraded in the cheap, bitter shell of my manhood. My manhood! How I loathed being a man, with its fierce responsibility... How I hated strength and duty and steadfastness. How I dreaded seeing my lovely sister with her damaged wrists and tubes running down her nose and the bottles of glucose hanging like glass embryos above her bed. But I knew my role so clearly now, knew the tyranny and the snare of maleness, and I would walk toward my sister as a pillar of strength... Strength was my gift; it was also my act, and I'm sure it's what will end up killing me. (55)

If courage is grace under pressure, Tom Wingo is a coward; there is nothing graceful about his conduct in the season of tumult that follows. As Dr. Lowenstein tries to help, Tom responds with mawkish surliness about being a South Carolinian in New York; he announces himself a "feminist football coach" who seethes with hostility against feminists. Yet Tom's obnoxious harangues have a constructive side. They are a parody of the male code of self-possessed self-reliance, and making a fool of himself makes him emotionally tangible. However noisy the process, Tom works his way out of his silent disassociated malice. A crucial form of courage, insufficiently honored among men, supports Tom's capacity to relinquish his self-command temporarily, in order to find an enlarged masculine competence.

The Prince of Tides, like *Affliction* and *Fargo,* dramatizes the need to realize patterns of manliness that transcend the maladies that are built into the conventional role. Tom's affliction, like that of Wade Whitehouse, is an extreme version of the damage most boys sustain at the hands of those who train them to become men. Tom seeks to construct a maleness that is active, salty, and compassionate, distinct from the isolation that permits Rolfe to avoid doing harm. Unlike Norm Gunderson, Tom is combative; he forcefully intervenes when he sees his loved ones at risk.

My point is not that Tom Wingo is a better "man" than Rolfe and Norm. The three narratives share a compelling diagnosis of the challenge that must be met in opening a landscape on which a variety of democratic manhoods can flourish. Two of these narratives were successful as novels, and all three were successful as films, which suggests a measure of improvement on the bed-and-board frontier. For a significant minority, at least, the horizons of gender have opened to include new manhoods capable of resisting the fascination of sexual violence and of forming relationships of egalitarian intimacy with women.

The disaster that overwhelms Wade Whitehouse and the redemption of Tom Wingo bring a core paradox into focus. Both Wade and Tom grew up passionately attached to their abusive fathers and secured (temporarily) the passionate attachment of the women they abused. Both exemplify the power of a terroristic relationship misrecognized as love.

In *Loving to Survive*, Dee Graham sees far-reaching significance in the "Stockholm Syndrome," so named because hostages taken in a 1973 Stockholm bank robbery gave their loyalty to the robber, reorganizing their emotional lives to serve his needs and endorse his purposes. The hostages ardently defended their captor to the police and to their own parents, whom they blamed for refusing to obey the robber's demands, which was tantamount—in their transformed vision—to holding them hostage. Passionately delusional, they blamed the police and their parents for preventing them from going home to be with their children. The terrifying cruelty of the robber became invisible to them, as did their own anger.

Graham argues that this transaction, in which victims identify with their victimizers, explains the adulation of abused children for their parents, and of abused women for the abusive men with whom they are intimate. Graham's theory of "chronic interpersonal abuse" illuminates the culture of male violence I have been describing, in particular the legacy of male cruelty that passes from one generation to the next (as abused boys internalize the "manhood" of their abusers) and the romantic mystifications practiced by women whose access to economic resources depends on retaining the favor of abusive men.[2]

This syndrome likewise helps to explain why "love" is generally considered the province of women, rather than men, with a huge industry churning out advice to women about how to show "love" in a way that secures a grip on masculine affections. Emotionally stunted men readily become addicted to this simulacrum, whether pornographic or not; and both parties may accept the mutual masquerade without recognizing the reciprocal cynicism and despair that lie at its heart. Wade Whitehouse and Tom Wingo interrupt the uncanny staleness of their intimate lives through outbursts of violence or exercises in venomous withdrawal, making contact with the cruelty and overruling domination at the core of their relationships. Such moments of living terror provide fleeting contact with emotional reality, but doom their intimates to maintaining the masquerade or canceling the relationship outright.

What's needed at the bed-and-board frontier is love, incorporating justice and truth, for which men bear responsibility equally with women. In *Democracy Begins between Two,* Luce Irigaray cautions against ceding the ethics of sexuality and family life to the religious right. She argues that principles of democratic equality should be pursued in intimate relations, and conversely, that "a real democracy must take as its basis, today, a just relationship between man and woman" (118).

Pursuing this thesis into a sustained discussion of issues in contemporary American society, bell hooks observes that love works against the "cultures of domination" that ensure obedience through fear and grant prescriptive rights of supremacy to whites or males (93). In *All About Love: New Visions,* hooks notes that the long-standing ethical and spiritual concern about love has been shunted aside by the obsessions of our commercial culture. Learning to love, as a deliberate practice, requires no expensive appliances; nor does it serve—as violence and pornography serve—to capture the attention of potential consumers. Precious few media outlets or advertising campaigns feature persons engaged in the disciplined and patient work—the discernment, communication, and action—that builds enduring love between husband and wife, or between same-sex partners, and provides a healthy context in which children can grow up self-respecting. Nor do questions of social justice sell advertising time (or advertising space) as predictably as sex scandals and violence. "Greed and exploitation become the norm when an ethic of domination prevails. They bring in their wake alienation and lovelessness. Intense spiritual and emotional lack in our lives is the perfect breeding ground for material greed and overconsumption" (105). "To know love," hooks declares, "we must surrender our attachment to sexist thinking in whatever form it takes in our lives" (155); her meditations offer assistance to anyone taking up that effort.[3]

The Art of Loving (1956), Erich Fromm's neglected classic, inaugurated a postwar discussion of love that coordinates psychological insight with social criticism, to define love as "union under the condition of preserving one's integrity," requiring the passionate and dedicated exercise of "care, responsibility, respect, and knowledge" (20–26). Fromm also provided a mid-twentieth-century analysis of the spiritual destruction entailed by capitalism, in the tradition of egalitarian critique I have traced from the late eighteenth century, to Henry David Thoreau in the mid-nineteenth century, and into the debates about imperialism, corporate capitalism, and manhood that extend from high-Victorian America into the present. The cravings of alienated and commodified souls are allayed but never satisfied by purchases, Fromm notes, but create a persistent consumerist mania, in which "the world is one great object for our appetite, a big apple, a big breast" (87), while substantive injustices of gender, class, race, and imperial domination vanish from public awareness.

At the same time, the movement toward gender justice has sources in the new economy, where middle-class households increasingly require the support of two incomes. This has created access for women to sectors of the workforce formerly monopolized by men; and the growing importance of "knowledge workers" has placed a premium on intellectual and technical skills that women can readily acquire. A new generation of men has been reared in households where parents share in childrearing and breadwinning.

Advances in the psychological understanding of manhood—led by Terrence Real, Ronald Levant, William Pollack, and Gary Brooks—presuppose households in which women are empowered to press men to develop the "relational" capacities that training to code manhood discourages. A fine literature is now becoming available for parents who want to raise what Pollack calls "real boys," free from the destructive consequences of code manhood and emotionally equipped to form mature loving relationships on egalitarian terms.

The anti-rape and anti-battering activism of the 1970s is another source from which the counterculture of male transformation has gained strength. Efforts to build a national movement have been balked by the conservative atmosphere of recent decades; in the 1990s membership in the National Organization of Men Against Sexism (NOMAS) fell below a thousand (Rhode 229) and the Oakland Men's Project has recently closed as an sponsor of gatherings, in order to concentrate on educational programs in communities and schools. Instead of a "movement" we have a fluctuating culture of ad hoc local organizations: Men Stopping Violence (Atlanta), D.C. Men Against Rape, Harvard Anti-sexist Men, Men Overcoming Violence (San Francisco), Men Stopping Rape (Madison, Wisconsin), Men Working to End Sexism and Violence (Halifax, Nova Scotia), Men Overcoming Abusive Behavior (Santa Cruz), Men to End

Sexual Assault (Cambridge). Organizations not devoted explicitly to men's concerns provide opportunities for what R. W. Connell calls "alliance politics" (*Masculinities* 238). Men and women working together on racial justice, welfare reform, environmental issues, educational reform, and economic justice find contexts in which to confront and work through the damage inflicted by sexism.

Gay male activism is likewise a significant force in the reconsideration of masculinity. Men who are targets of homophobia have an experience strongly analogous to that of women victimized by sexual misogyny: both are abused by men seeking to bolster traditional manhood. "Macho men are far more complex than they want to realize," remarked James Baldwin in 1984. "They have needs which, for them, are literally inexpressible. They don't dare look into the mirror. And that is why they need faggots. They've created faggots in order to act out a sexual fantasy on the body of another man and not take any responsibility for it" (Katz 104).

Gay masculinities are not *ipso facto* egalitarian, but there is no reason they cannot be. The experience of same-sex couples—male and female—who fashion households that do not match the traditional gender hierarchy, promises to generate new understandings of loving mutuality. Such households may also provide a context for childrearing practices that do not instill despotic manhood or its female correlates.

The conceptual tools needed to refashion male gendering are being developed by scholars in a wide range of fields within and outside the academy. These writers don't all agree with one another, but taken together they amount to a significant development in contemporary gender history. They represent centers of study nationwide, where conversations go forward—men with men and women with men—discussing the maladies of male gendering, seeking more humane alternatives, and defining the social changes needed to foster them. This is not the same thing as a massive social movement, visualized as football stadiums full of enthusiasts, boulevards full of marchers, or a data bank of voters and contributors, but it is not without promise.

It is shortsighted to dismiss the work of academics in the humanities and social sciences as ivory-tower theorizing, of consequence only to other academics. Throughout our history there have been eras when the movement toward gender justice has surged up. Given a coherent focus by articulate and well-informed leadership, it rises above the horizon of public awareness and achieves worthwhile political goals. But the insight that informs these efforts is not generated on the spot, and the collective awareness that sustains them accumulates in long periods of quiet preparation. It would be folly to predict that we are on the verge of a major new attack on sexual violence strongly supported by men. But it would be equally foolish to imagine that such a moment will never arrive. The male profeminist countercurrent traceable through William Sanger and Theodore Dwight Weld has now become a counterculture, offering companionship in the quest and providing insights that will serve the cause in the long term.

The miseries caused by the rape and battering of women arise from a male-supremacist social ethos long antedating the

United States, one that now has woven itself into the articulation of democratic ideals, provides support to our economic arrangements and our international ambitions, and is perpetuated through childrearing practices that start to work on small boys and girls before they can toddle. Understanding the historical processes that have yielded the twenty-first-century forms of American sexism entails telling a story that provides ample precedents for the cruelties visited upon women today. And this may seem like an invitation to despair, especially when we consider the ideologically confident tide of male-supremacist reaction that is now running through our religious and political institutions, with powerful representatives in the media.

It is necessary to avoid the trap of atrocity quietism, the paralyzing conclusion that nothing of value can be done unless a wholesale renovation of American society can be achieved forthwith. Henry David Thoreau described the quiet desperation that drives American men to seek consolation in abusive sexuality, and he focused his quest for a remedy on a small-scale project. Building a little house on Walden pond provided him a new vantage from which to view the social landscape of the 1840s, and his example has continued to aid men who seek redemption. "We must learn to re-awaken and keep ourselves awake," Thoreau declared; we must stay awake in the darkness "by an infinite expectation of the dawn" (62).

Men dedicated to breaking the cycle of violence have at hand dozens of worthwhile enterprises. Support is needed for the panoply of efforts that offer women protection: women's shelters, rape crisis intervention agencies, educational programs in schools, police forces, and emergency rooms. It is also urgent to enlarge the resources available to men taking up "men's work," the task of identifying and seeking to surmount the sexist violence within their own socialization and in the institutions by which that socialization continues to deform the souls of growing boys.[4] The bed-and-board frontier, on which gender equality needs to make headway, is no less challenging for being close at hand. Yet the work of love in our intimate relations must grow together with a renewal of the ethical awareness we bring to public life. A democratic standard, recognizing the equal worth and dignity of every person, provides the measure against which the ethos of domination must be opposed as we encounter it in the workplace, in religious institutions, in the entertainment industry, and in political affairs.

Epilogue

I WANT TO RETURN to the moment in Waldo, Florida, when I first responded with fascination to pornographic violence. I said in the Prologue that historical and cultural patterns of gendering had entered the formation of my boyhood, and incipient manhood, to set me up for this moment. But how?

Going to the railway station with my parents brought back the emotional turmoil of the war years, which included my father's departure from the home when I was five. "Now you're the man of the house," he said, only half joking. "Take good care of your mother." My mother opposed his going off to war, but only later did I discern this; nothing was said about their conflict in my presence, then or ever. The ensuing years were difficult for her, and she praised me lavishly for helping.

I did not imagine then—nor do I believe today—that he joined the navy in order to get away from us, any more than he went to work because he preferred his life at the office to being at home. He went to war without complaining, and against his own desire, so that we could be safe and provided for. By age five I knew that the swastika was a Nazi emblem, and I remember telling him my discovery: if I pressed my fingertips against my closed eyelids I could "see" swastikas rotating and coming toward me. I thought this was a curious fact—well worth relating—and was startled at my father's face going pale. I've wondered since whether that moment entered his decision to get into the war.

I have many memories of my father as a naval officer, handsome in his uniform as he boarded the trains that took him away, with the huge navy-issue suitcase lightly balanced on his shoulder. He had a relatively easy service. Hoping to ship as a communications officer on a destroyer, he was picked out to study Russian, was assigned to the National Security Group, and served out the balance of the war in Washington, D.C., where we all lived together. As a second grader, I had a friend across the street whose father had won the Congressional Medal of Honor, which we were allowed reverentially to inspect. I remember feeling sad that this medal, in its velvet-lined box, was all that remained of his dad.

The most powerful of my wartime memories took place after the war was over and we had moved to Florida, where my father had begun to teach Shakespeare. We were thrilled when Laurence Olivier's *Henry V* came to the local movie house, and my father prepared us by reading and explaining excerpts from the play. One speech struck directly home to me; I wept over it after I went to bed that night. It is Prince Hal exhorting his troops before the battle of Agincourt, which takes place on St. Crispian's day:

> This story shall the good man teach his son;
> And Crispin Crispian shall ne'er go by,
> From this day to the ending of the world,
> But we in it shall be remembered,—
> We few, we happy few, we band of brothers;
> For he to-day that sheds his blood with me
> Shall be my brother; be he ne'er so vile,
> This day shall gentle his condition:
> And gentlemen in England now a-bed
> Shall think themselves accurst they were not here;
> And hold their manhoods cheap whiles any speaks
> That fought with us upon St. Crispin's day. (IV.iii.56–67)

This moment caught together currents of passion—of dread, love, grief, loyalty, rage, and aspiration—that passed between my father and me. The lesson that it taught lay beyond words, even Shakespeare's words; it was a lesson about what I had suffered, explaining why he had gone away, possibly to die. It was also about what I would be required to suffer, and the stoical self-containment with which my sufferings would have to be borne. Masculine honor—my father's honor—demanded no less.

In later years I discovered that my father had received a letter from his father as he prepared to go to war. "No use to express my grief that your long-cherished plans and present happy domestic and professional situation may be interrupted for a while," my grandfather wrote. "God knows, I wish I could take your place and go into it instead of you, and let you stay where you are. But since the warmakers do not come at us with their old men, we cannot meet them with our old men. Our young men are needed in their homes and work—and we old fellows who are practically through ought to do the scrapping."

Behind this whimsical humor lay the iron rule, binding father and son. Shirking service was to them unthinkable. Equally unthinkable was complaining about it.

My mother's opposition was no less strong for being covert. Her closest friend was living in Tokyo, married to a Japanese man; to her the coming of war was a nightmare of madness, horror, and lies. Yet the prevailing ethos taught that it was appropriate for a woman to feel such distresses, and for a man to discount them. I do not believe that his decision to enter the war was a mistake; the injustice lay in his overruling her objections, rather than engaging them fully.

My father's departure for the war intensified a state of things that would have been present in any event. Both of my parents had weaknesses and made mistakes; like all parents, they bequeathed emotional liabilities to their children. But the maladies of manhood I've sought to understand in this book were equally instilled by what they had reason to look upon as their virtues. His were the masculine virtues of command and self-command; hers were the womanly virtues of self-sacrificing household nurture.

To all exterior appearances they adored each other, and in truth their love was strong; but it bridged over unspoken anger and grief. My mother resented subordination, and sought to fulfill fierce ambitions through her sons; my father's occasional fury counteracted the pain of his isolation from the rest of us. For quite different reasons, each sought to keep these chronic torments locked down, so that the tenor of household life sometimes took on a formal tone. A dignified minuet of gestures and diplomatic double meanings worked to conceal the emotional suffering.

Looking back two generations to my father and grandfather, I also look forward two generations to my son and grandson. Much of what I've inherited I hope to have passed along intact, in particular the fatherly caring that sees more value in a "happy domestic and professional situation" than in the prospect of battlefield glory. But I hope to have interrupted the gender tradition treated in this book, the ideal of manhood that encloses an internal contradiction, according to which strong, independent, well-educated women were admired yet expected to accept subordination gracefully. In this book I seek to understand the psychosocial forces that make this contradiction seem like common sense, so their power can be broken.

At age twelve my wartime terrors had subsided, as had the consciousness of bearing masculine duties I was unfit to perform. Yet I was restless in the Waldo train station because being there awakened old anxieties that now underlay dilemmas that were new to me. I had not really been expected to "be a man" when I was five; otherwise I myself would have gone away to war. But now the experience of manhood was pressing in upon me. Memories of departures and temporary homecomings at train stations brought back the obligation to "take it like a man" when besieged by severe distress, never voicing openly my anguish, rage, and terror.

This code entailed fierce unconscious resistance to my rapidly emerging adult sexuality. The surges of desire that accompanied my fascination with the bodies of my schoolmates felt like attacks on my self-respect, and the "nice" girls conspired with my effort to pretend I felt no such thing. I myself did not feel "nice," and I felt a resentment-laden sexual fascination with the "not nice" girls to whom I felt secretly akin. These vexations were more than I could manage, and fantasies of sexual coercion helped me bolster my illusion of all-mastering manliness. Looking back, I can see that my emotional life conformed to the whore/angel dichotomy long before I'd ever heard of it. At the time I hardly knew what I was feeling, since I was discouraged by the ethos of manhood from exploring my emotional life.

The image, in the Spillane paperback, of a helpless naked woman being lashed with a leather belt dramatized what lay behind the wall of my self-ignorance. It was an image of what I was doing to myself, as well as of what I wanted to do. This sordid fantasy was the armature of a manhood that was to me the essence of human dignity, a noble self-sacrifice floating like a banner above the convulsion of desire, grief, and rage that was my inner battleground.

I was shamed by the cruelty and dehumanization of the scene; and although I had never heard the term "misogyny," I knew that the scenario depicted a wrong against women that should cancel my fascination *de novo*. But these moral admonitions were automatically drawn into the masculine ethos of conscientious self-command that had produced the anxiety and the compensatory "lust" in the first place. The culture of manhood that had shaped my inner life required the repression of involuntary sexual feelings, since these were forbidden by the masculine self-image I felt duty-bound to maintain. The result was a pervasive sexual anxiety, a restive conjunction of yearning and self-punishment that was all the more helpless because unconscious.

The Spillane scenario triggered a surge of desire because it provided a drama that organized the components of my inward dilemma: it provided a commanding masculine presence to identify with, secure in a belted raincoat and wholly in control; it provided a frightened and sexually aroused woman who played out the sexual panic that I could not discern as my own; and however entangled in this cruel interaction, it portrayed desire itself. The scene satisfied in fantasy my resentment against women who aroused me against my will, by placing me in the role of punisher; it also played out the punishment I chronically inflicted upon myself. The "man" whipping the "woman" enacted the masculinity I aspired to, as it inflicted punitive discipline on a "feminine" sexual impulsiveness that it could never subdue. The desire depicted and provoked by the scenario was thus doubly sanctioned: it was experienced even as it was being punished, and it was under the control of a self-possessed man.

Yet my investment in the scenario of pornographic violence also expressed a yearning for self-knowledge. I unconsciously wanted to reclaim as my own the feelings that were portrayed by the aroused and terrified woman, so that I perceived in the fantasy, albeit dimly, the promise of a larger acquaintance with my own life. The syndrome of pornographic enchantment perpetuated itself because it was fueled by the anxiety that followed in its wake, but it was likewise fueled by my intuition that the syndrome touched an emotional truth in myself that I desperately needed to see clearly and accept as my own. At the core of this truth, however obscured by the prohibitions of my socialization into manhood and the fantasy life to which they led, was a strong and healthy sexual responsiveness of which I had no reason to be ashamed.

There is a dialectic within sexually coercive fantasy: along a vector of self-ignorance the core anxieties generating the fantasy remain concealed, leading toward exploitation and abuse. But there is also a vector of self-knowledge, pointing toward the distresses that are compensated by the spell. Moving along that vector involves acknowledging the personal and social sources of those distresses and undoing the abusive pattern of desire that results from keeping them hidden. Following the vector of self-knowledge can lead to greater mutual knowledge in intimate relationships, enhancing their intimacy and the sexual fulfillments they offer.[1]

The moment in the Waldo train station marked my entrance into a pornographic sensibility that was at odds with the dominant themes of American popular culture in the 1950s but that has since become ubiquitous in middle-of-the road films and advertising. Contemporary media representations provide a wealth of outward sexual images that focus and enact our anxieties, inviting us to displace anger and inner pain. Instead of engaging the emotional truth that lies behind our fantasies, contemporary advertising and film offer an enchanted kingdom in which we can escape from our emotional troubles and find temporary relief, only to have those troubles resume their force unimpaired once the spell has worn off.

As a means for selling products to consumers, this addictive process is not only useful to companies marketing pornography; it is useful to any corporation whose retail products can be linked to "sex." When we condemn "consumerism" we focus on the gullibility of the public, without sufficiently recognizing the cynical cunning of advertising campaigns that exploit the emotional liabilities of potential customers and strengthen those liabilities so as to keep the addiction alive, perpetuating the delusion that making purchases can resolve our most stubborn moral conflicts.[2]

Still, the need to find integrity and self-knowledge is a potent force in our lives, and it too plays a part in what draws us to pornographic enchantments. Like most men who are captivated by fantasies of sexual coercion in their early teenage years, I was able to refrain from acting on abusive impulses, which set me apart from young men destined for careers as harassers and rapists. But I was not able to refrain from having such impulses, or from harboring a covert fellow feeling for men who act them out.

This guilty sympathy was to a degree sustained by illusion, however, since sexual abuse is a transaction quite different from what is usually envisioned in pornographic fantasies, as rapists themselves sometimes discover. In working on this book I viewed a videotape of a convicted offender who was asked whether the assault had in fact fulfilled his fantasy. "No," he replied with bland inhumanity. "The whole deal was much too hectic." Pornographic fantasies lead a man to surround accounts of rape with an aura of unreality—as though such things don't happen to real people. A law-abiding man hearing a victim's testimony is all too likely to route it into the fantasy zone and find it hard to believe that such a thing actually took place. All too familiar with scenes of sexual coercion in his fantasy life, the man is disoriented and at a loss when abuse is presented as happening in fact.

We need to understand our surges of prurient interest in real-world terms: to see them as symptoms of inner anxiety. We need to step back from such moments and reclaim the projections, owning our gendered predicament and knowing directly the distress it entails. We need to find the courage to bear such disconcerting emotional states—and to read their social and personal meanings accurately—instead of resorting to the self-deception of experiencing them vicariously, through fantasies of a victimized "woman."

At the small college where I teach we have registration in the gym, professors sitting side by side at long tables as the students form lines to sign up for our courses. I was gazing out across the gym floor, recently, when I realized that I had fixed a predatory gaze on a woman student in a yellow tee shirt. I did not know the student: my fascination had nothing to do with her as a person. In the instant I deliberately looked away, and turned my attention to other matters. But the image stayed in my mind, returning to consciousness as registration wound down and persisting for an hour or two afterward. The source of this pornographic enchantment lay in myself, not in the student, but where? Slowly it dawned on me that I had grown increasingly anxious during registration, as my younger colleagues had more applicants for their courses than I had for mine. The placating considerations—my courses were at unattractive hours, for example—did nothing to quell the dread of having lost my popularity with students by reason of age, with its creeping incapacity, its falling out of touch with contemporary excitements, to say nothing of inferior teaching. These are not trivial considerations, and I need to face them. I found them waiting for me when I worked my way to the sources of my pornographic fascination instead of accepting it as inseparable from being a man.

The anxieties of the moment had awakened the compulsion to self-command, silencing impulsive and unpredictable emotional responses, especially sexual responses. For the sake of a restive equilibrium I had attacked my own strength. To be sexually alive, to be warmed and charmed and delighted, is a source not only of innocent pleasure but also of the vitality that sustains long-range creative enterprises. The pretty young student might have afforded a moment of blessing, rather than becoming the target of an embarrassed and persistent fantasy of sexual conquest.

A wealth of human fulfillment opens up when a man learns to break the spell that reduces women to compensatory intoxicants. Learning to break that spell is itself a phenomenon of wealth. It musters the legacy of caring and commitment that kept us alive as children, which is reinforced and enlarged by those who come to love us, and to criticize us honestly, in our adult lives. The measures of compassion and fair play that we receive through work and community involvements also contribute their store to the courage that sustains us. Across this complex personal and social landscape we bear an obligation to truth-telling, to justice, and to love, because the loudest voices in our society tell quite a different story. The stereotypical sex goddess, in endless media avatars, is a caricature of sex. It replaces the sexual initiatives of women with an effort to elicit the pornographic fascination of men, and it encourages men to remain ignorant of chronic masculine terrors, including those awakened by sexual desire itself. The determination to undo the sexual pathologies that bedevil women and men opens a large agenda of reflection and hard work, but it promises a world in which we can meet one another, and touch one another, and look at the truth together.

Notes

Works Cited

Acknowledgments

Index

Notes

1. Frontiers of Masculinity

1 A major turning point came with Joseph Pleck's critique of "male sex role identity" theory, which held that men have problems attaining a sex role thought to be ordained by their maleness, and his development of the "gender role strain paradigm," which holds that gender roles are socially constructed and impose systemic strains. Pleck reviews the development of this theory in "The Gender Role Strain Paradigm." The sociological works of Brod, Connell, Kaufman, and Kimmel incorporate this view, as do the historical and literary studies of Kimmel, Leverenz, and Rotundo. Psychoanalytic approaches to the emotional suffering imposed by conventional models of manhood have been developed by Brooks, Levant, William Pollack, Real, and Silverberg. Works focusing on the issue of sexual abuse include Brooks, "Centerfold Syndrome"; Brooks and Silverstein, "Understanding the Dark Side"; and Lisak, "Male Gender Socialization."

2 See Levant and Brooks, "Introduction," in *Men and Sex,* 2. Samuel Osherson, often with telling insight into male pain,

underemphasizes the requirements of gender justice. He characterizes "hypermasculinity," "the pre-emptive strike," and "disdain and ridicule" as "creative strategies" men use to cope with their inner misery (111–121) and dismisses issues of economic power as a "red herring" (174). Looking to the future, William S. Pollack and Ronald F. Levant speak of the need for an approach "empathic to male development" that is "gender-sensitive and aware and respectful of women's needs and rights as well" ("Coda," 383).

3 The expression "hegemonic masculinity" has gained currency as a way of referring to the model of manhood treated in this book. Connell provides an extensive and illuminating analysis, noting that "hegemonic" describes a social relation between dominant and subordinated groups, following Antonio Gramsci's discussion of class relations, which stresses the concessions that the rulers must make to the ruled and the stake that the ruled acquire in the social arrangement that holds them subject (67–86). Sherry Ortner, in "Gender Hegemonies," applies this doctrine to the situation of women and men in cultures around the world. Connell defines hegemonic masculinity as "the configuration of gender practice which embodies the currently accepted answer to the problem of the legitimacy of patriarchy" (77).

These are astute and compelling sociological observations, and I have no quarrel with the value-free language in which they are framed. It is evident that American women continue to accommodate themselves to patriarchal social arrangements, and for the most part view the patriarchy as legitimate. Were this not the case, the voting power of women established in 1920 would long since have abolished male dominance.

But in this book I seek a place among the unreconciled, women and men who oppose patriarchy outright; and the ethically loaded terms of the late eighteenth-century democratic revolutions serve this purpose. The term "despotic" may sound antique, but the democratic principles that gave it meaning are still relevant today. Encouraging the development of "democratic masculinities," requires asserting *de novo* that "the legitimacy of the patriarchy" is a figment of illegitimate power, no matter how much ingenuity may be expended in promoting it.

4 Karen Horney's *The Neurotic Personality of Our Time* and *Feminine Psychology* pioneered this tradition and emphasized the psychic damage produced by conventions of male dominance. Jerome Frank and Julia Frank, in *Persuasion and Healing*, demonstrated that psychic maladies as well as their treatment are defined by the conceptions of humanity that a given society instills. More recent studies emphasize the role of "culture," incorporating Clifford Geertz's view of culture as a system of meanings in whose terms our selves are fashioned. Arthur Kleinman's *Rethinking Psychiatry* offers a cross-cultural investigation, while Michael Cole's *Cultural Psychology* provides a general survey of this impulse within psychology. The program of investigation led by Jerome Bruner—and sketched in his *The Culture of Education*—further indicates the scope of this enterprise.

5 Daly and Wilson discuss the debates occasioned by their discovery of this effect (83–93). Hrdy argues that reduced altruism accounts for such infanticide in humans, in contrast to the purposeful removal of nongenetic offspring found in other mammals (235–249).

2. Rape as an Activity of the Imagination

1 The connection between Whitman's vision of democracy and his celebration of same-sex desire is illuminated by Christopher Newfield in "Democracy and Male Homoeroticism," an extensive discussion of the ways in which homophobia serves antidemocratic hierarchies that have "become a cornerstone of our ongoing system of administered democracy" (30). As with misogyny, so with homophobia: both have been perpetuated as inherent to American freedom, even as they violate the ideal.

2 Betsy Erkkila observes that this "union seems less the occasion for a dynamic pairing of equals and more the scene of a domestic rape," and notes the 1883 comment of Elizabeth Cady Stanton that Whitman "speaks as if the female must be forced to the creative act, apparently ignorant of the great natural fact that a healthy woman has as much passion as a man" (138). Michael Moon treats this poem in discussing Whitman's negotiation of the conceptions of bodiliness emerging in his culture, noting that it emphasizes women's "lack" even as it proclaims their self-sufficiency (96–97). Vivian Pollack concludes that this poem, and Whitman's treatment of women generally, makes claims to "empower women" while "reinscribing them within fixed social roles in which they are always potentially subordinated to men ("In Loftiest," 92), and in *The Erotic Whitman* she situates this strategy biographically, within the underlying anxieties of Whitman's sexual life.

3 Roy Hazelwood, a pioneer of the FBI's program of criminal investigative analysis, discusses these issues in *Dark Dreams*.

4 At times rapists may derive a specious validation of their beliefs from the presence of vaginal lubrication, and victims as a result may take on increased guilt. But neither the vindication nor the guilt is justified: the violation of a woman's sexual autonomy is intensified, not diminished, if the assault calls forth unwanted physiological responses. See the discussion provided by Slava Ellis in Beneke, *Men on Rape,* 133–135.

5 The force of this dynamism in nineteenth-century American literary culture is demonstrated by Glenn Hendler, who in "Tom Sawyer's Masculinity" treats the genre of the "bad boys book" as relying on the claim that "radical self-loss is the prerequisite for the attainment of normative masculinity" (46).

6 Simone de Beauvoir launched the contemporary discussion of the woman as "Other" in *The Second Sex,* and the protocols of the self-other relationship govern homophobia as well as misogyny. The literature that treats the psychosocial and ethical issues of same-sex desire, and of the injustices suffered by gays and lesbians, casts light on the question of male sexual violence against women.

Just as manhood is defined oppositionally as "not-womanhood," so heterosexuality is defined as "not-homosexual," and in each case the two terms of the polarity are interdefining. These polarities serve a structure of social domination, such that the ruling definitions are ostensibly those of "man" and "heterosexual," but a compelling logic shows that the significance of these ruling terms is in fact given by their opposites, such that "man" and "heterosexual" are in fact constituted by their opposites. The violence dealt out to women and to homosexual men, accordingly, works in part to quash awareness of this fact because such an awareness will destabilize the entire mythos. On the logic of the "other" as applied differentially to male-female and male-male desire, see Michael Warner, "Homo-Narcissism; or, Heterosexuality."

7 In *After the Lovedeath,* Lawrence Kramer provides a compelling series of meditations on the internal dynamics and high-cultural articulations of the gender structure that defines womanhood and manhood to be polar opposites, and argues eloquently for a "gender synergy," to transcend the systemic sexual violence that results (12).

8 On Ahab's self-loathing and hatred of the whale as related to the gender conflicts inherent to self-possessed masculinity, see David Leverenz, *Manhood and the American Renaissance,* esp. 279–281, 287–297.

9 The quotations come from a tape to which Ed Richards gave me access. See also Michaud, 211.

10 This view of the "inner feminine" also entered Freudian theory, as Joseph Pleck observes, largely through the work of Felix Boehm and Karen Horney in the 1930s. This tradition of interpretation envisions not a harmony of "masculine" and "feminine" traits but a ceaseless struggle of the "masculine" to fend off the "feminine" (*Myth of Masculinity* 157). For Jung's view see "Anima and Animus"; see also "Rex and Regina," in *Mysterium Coniunctionis.*

11 Donovan discusses Fuller and the leaders at Seneca Falls as exponents of an "Enlightenment Liberal Feminism," whose recent versions have aroused controversy (1–30). The term "equal rights feminists" has been applied to women who are charged with seeking equality with upper-middle-class men without recognizing the oppression of women on which their

privileges depend (see hooks, *Ain't,* 119–158; Newman, 184–185). Yet Donovan demonstrates that key terms of this early tradition remain vital today.

3. *Becoming a Natural Man*

1 Warrior manhood has long coexisted with less boastful forms. In *Manhood and the American Renaissance,* David Leverenz shows that a patrician form of manhood was available in early nineteenth-century America to the landed gentry, and to merchants, lawyers, and clergy who possessed wealth (preferably inherited) and social position; while master craftsmen and journeymen, like shipboard officers and plantation overseers, claimed an artisan manhood based on advanced skill in their occupations and on the independence it provided (72–107). Anthony Rotundo's *American Manhood* and Michael Kimmel's *Manhood in America* demonstrate the existence of multiple styles that have changed as American history unfolded, and R. W. Connell's *Masculinities* treats the social formation of distinct manhoods in the late twentieth century. John Stoltenberg's *Refusing to be a Man* celebrates the struggle of gay men who defy the exclusive claims of warrior manhood, and Terrence Real's *I Don't Want to Talk about It* illustrates the toxic effects of the warrior ideal in the lives of straight men. Religious grounds for the cultivation of alternative manhoods are present in the Jewish tradition, as outlined in Daniel Boyarin's splendid *Unheroic Conduct.* Christian traditions useful to this end are treated in Stephen Boyd, *The Men We Yearn to Be.*

2 Russ Castronovo, in *Fathering the Nation,* delineates the exclusionary model of masculinity that was identified with

the antebellum "national narrative." The identification between white masculinity and public life persisted throughout the nineteenth century, accumulating erotic meanings
that Glenn Hendler discusses in "Pandering in the Public
Sphere."

3 On this double pattern within American social history see
Sellers (esp. chs. 1 and 13) and Wiebe (esp. chs. 1, 4, 6, 10). Alexander and Mohanty also distinguish between the democratic
promise of equal rights for all and the monopoly upon that
promise asserted by U.S. capitalism and imperialism (xxvii–
xlii).

4. Pornographic Manhood

1 Frank Rich reports that the porn industry has continued to
proliferate in the decade since the Margold interview, largely
through a greatly enlarged market that embraces the Internet,
videocassettes, and X-rated films for rent on hotel movie
channels. Rich indicates that the business totals annually between $10 billion and $14 billion in the United States, and
points out that if the correct figure is $10 billion, "pornogra-
phy is a bigger business than professional football, basketball,
and baseball put together" (51). In a related article Kristin
Hohenadel notes that serious filmmakers are beginning to ex-
periment with shots of penetration and other representations
of explicit sex, "as the home delivery of pornography by way
of the Internet and cable television becomes more routine"
(1). There remains a consequential distinction between works
depicting explicit sexual conduct and those celebrating coercion. Hohenadel reports that among the new offerings is the
"feminist intellectual cinema" of Catherine Beillat. Evidence

that endorsement of sexual abuse is an enduring feature of sexually explicit material generally can be found in Blue Moon Books—offering such titles as *The Ravishing of Leslie* and *Captive I, Captive II, Captive III, Captive IV,* which follow *The Story of O* in seeking an upscale market.

2 For excellent discussions see Mary Ryan on "prudent procreators" in *Cradle of the Middle Class,* 180, and Charles Sellers, "Ethos vs. Eros," in *Market Revolution,* ch. 8.

3 Dimmesdale's suffering, the penalty for his failure to uphold the standard of code manhood, works here to confirm that standard rather than undermine it, an instance of the hegemonic feminization that Christopher Newfield locates at the heart of Dimmesdale's character. In "The Politics of Male Suffering," Newfield demonstrates that masculine submissiveness, self-doubt, and masochism—traits marking a man as "feminine"—not only reassert the patriarchal code in theory but at the level of sexual politics generate an abundance of strategies for maintaining male supremacist authority.

6. *Rape as Redemption*

1 Mark Seltzer, in *Serial Killers,* cogently analyses a cultural logic that informs public depictions of serial murder in our own times as rooted in the emergence of a "machine" society in high-Victorian America, in which the mass public was served by a media apparatus creating celebrities. The notorious Chicago physician H. H. Holmes constructed a hundred-room "Murder Castle," with elaborate systematic procedures echoing those of the modern corporation, and Seltzer notes that Holmes may be viewed as "an extreme limit case of the self-made man" (8).

7. Democratic Masculinities

1 Ronald Levant observes that "the exclusive reliance on nonrelational sexuality is a state of being that is less than fully optimal in today's world, where men must meet women on an equal plane" ("Nonrelational" 14). But this is true only in very limited regions of "today's world" where women have obtained economic and political power sufficient to counteract traditional arrangements, as Levant notices in remarking that "the social changes wrought by the feminist movement and the influx of women into the workforce have left our traditional code of masculinity in a state of collapse" (*Masculinity* 1).

2 In *The Protestant Temperament*, Philip Greven describes the strongly analogous "will breaking" style of childrearing that was codified as an "evangelical" religious prescription among authoritarian families in early America, who trained their children to grateful obedience toward unquestioned authority. In *Spare the Child*, he demonstrates the persistence of this tradition in the twentieth century.

3 Augustus Napier, in *The Fragile Bond*, grounds a searching discussion on his effort to establish an "equal, intimate and enduring" relationship in his own marriage.

4 See Paul Kivel, *Men's Work: Facilitator's Guide*, as well as W. Pollack, Real, Kindlon and Thompson, Levant, Brooks.

Epilogue

1 Stephen Goldbart and David Wallin discuss the consensual enactment of aggressive fantasies within intimate relationships. They emphasize that healthy acting out, as opposed to

abusive acting out, requires fully informed and freely embraced mutual consent (33–38).

2 I am grateful to Tim Beneke for comments that led me to see this issue more clearly.

Works Cited

Abzug, Robert. *Cosmos Crumbling: American Reform and the Religious Imagination.* New York: Oxford University Press, 1994.

Adams, Abigail, and John Adams. *The Book of Abigail and John: Selected Letters of the Adams Family, 1762–1784.* Ed. L. H. Butterfield, Marc Friedlaender, and Mary-Jo Kline. Cambridge, Mass.: Harvard University Press, 1975.

Alexander, M. Jacqui, and Chandra Talpade Mohanty, eds. *Feminist Genealogies, Colonial Legacies, Democratic Futures.* New York: Routledge, 1997.

Appleby, Joyce. *Inheriting the Revolution: The First Generation of Americans.* Cambridge, Mass.: Harvard University Press, 2000.

Auerbach, Jonathan. *Male Call: Becoming Jack London.* Durham: Duke University Press, 1996.

Baldwin, James. "Everybody's Protest Novel." *Notes of a Native Son.* Boston: Beacon, 1957.

Banks, Russell. *Affliction.* New York: Harper, 1989.

Barker-Benfield, G. J. *The Horrors of the Half-Known Life: Male Attitudes toward Women and Sexuality in Nineteenth-Century America.* 2nd ed. New York: Routledge, 2000.

Basch, Norma. *In the Eyes of the Law: Women, Marriage, and Property in Nineteenth-Century New York.* London: Cornell University Press, 1982.

Bates, Milton J. *The Wars We Took to Vietnam: Cultural Conflict and Storytelling.* Berkeley: University of California Press, 1996.

Beauvoir, Simone de. *The Second Sex.* New York: Knopf, 1993.

Bederman, Gail. *Manliness and Civilization: A Cultural History of Gender and Race in the United States, 1880–1917.* Chicago: University of Chicago Press, 1995.

Benedict, Helen. *Virgin or Vamp: How the Press Covers Sex Crimes.* New York: Oxford University Press, 1992.

Beneke, Timothy. *Men on Rape: What They Have to Say about Sexual Violence.* New York: St. Martin's, 1982.

—— *Proving Manhood: Reflections on Men and Sexism.* Berkeley: University of California Press, 1997.

Boyarin, Daniel. *Unheroic Conduct: The Rise of Heterosexuality and the Invention of the Jewish Man.* Berkeley: University of California Press, 1997.

Boyd, Stephen B. *The Men We Long to Be: Beyond Lonely Warriors and Desperate Lovers.* 1995. Cleveland: Pilgrim, 1997.

Brod, Harry, ed. *The Making of Masculinities: The New Men's Studies.* New York: Routledge, 1987.

Brod, Harry, and Michael Kaufman, eds. *Theorizing Masculinities: Research on Men and Masculinities.* Newbury Park, Calif.: Sage, 1994.

Brooks, Gary R. "The Centerfold Syndrome: How Men Can Overcome Objectification and Achieve Intimacy with Women." *Men and Sex.* Ed. Levant and Brooks.

Brooks, Gary R., and L. B. Silverstein. "Understanding the Dark Side of Masculinity: An Integrative Systems Model." *New Psychology of Men.* Ed. Levant and Pollack.

Brownmiller, Susan. *Against Our Will: Men, Women and Rape.* New York: Bantam, 1975.

Bruner, Jerome. *The Culture of Education.* Cambridge, Mass.: Harvard University Press, 1996.

Burgess, Ann, et al. "Serial Rapists and Their Victims: Reenactment and Repetition." *Human Sexual Aggression: Current Perspectives.* Ed. Robert A. Prentky and Vernon L. Quinsey. Vol. 528. New York: New York Academy, 1987.

Cadick, Jerry. "On Being a Warrior." *Newsweek,* 14 April 1997: 14.

Carnes, Mark C. *Secret Ritual and Manhood in Victorian America.* New Haven: Yale University Press, 1989.

Castronovo, Russ. *Fathering the Nation: American Genealogies of Slavery and Freedom.* Berkeley: University of California Press, 1995.

Chudacoff, Howard. *The Age of the Bachelor: Creating an American Subculture.* Princeton: Princeton University Press, 1999.

Clover, Carol J. *Men, Women, and Chain Saws: Gender in the Modern Horror Film.* Princeton: Princeton University Press, 1992.

Cole, Michael. *Cultural Psychology: A Once and Future Discipline.* Cambridge, Mass.: Harvard University Press, 1996.

Coles, Robert. "Boys to Men." *New York Times Book Review,* 27 June 2000: 20.

Connell, R. W. *Masculinities.* Berkeley: University of California Press, 1995.

Conroy, Pat. *The Prince of Tides.* New York: Bantam, 1986.

Crane, Stephen. *The Red Badge of Courage.* 2nd ed. Ed. Sculley Bradley et al. New York: Norton, 1976.

Daly, Martin, and Margo Wilson. *Homicide.* New York: Aldine de Gruyter, 1988.

Darnton, Robert. *The Forbidden Best-Sellers of Pre-Revolutionary France.* New York: Norton, 1995.

—— "Sex for Thought." *New York Review of Books,* 22 Dec. 1994: 65–74.

Degler, Carl. *At Odds: Women and the Family in America from the Revolution to the Present.* New York: Oxford University Press, 1980.

Donovan, Josephine. *Feminist Theory: The Intellectual Traditions of American Feminism.* New York: Continuum, 1998.

Douglas, John, and Mark Olshaker. *Mindhunter: Inside the FBI's Elite Serial Crime Unit.* New York: Scribner, 1995.

Dutton, Donald, and Susan K. Golant. *The Batterer: A Psychological Profile.* New York: Basic Books, 1995.

Dworkin, Andrea. *Pornography: Men Possessing Women.* 1979. New York: Plume, 1989.

Dyer, Gwynne. *War.* New York: Crown, 1985.

Ehrenreich, Barbara. *Blood Rites: Origins and History of the Passions of War.* New York: Metropolitan, 1997.

Ellis, Bret Easton. *American Psycho.* New York: Vintage, 1991.

Emerson, Ralph Waldo. *Selections from Ralph Waldo Emerson: An Organic Anthology.* Boston: Houghton Mifflin, 1957.

Erkkila, Betsy. *Whitman the Political Poet.* New York: Oxford University Press, 1989.

Fargo. Dir. Joel Coen. Perf. Frances McDormand, William H. Macy, Steve Buscemi, and Harve Presnell. Polygram Video, 1996.

Feidelson, Charles, Jr. *Symbolism and American Literature.* Chicago: University of Chicago Press, 1953.

Fiedler, Leslie A. *Love and Death in the American Novel.* New York: Dell, 1960.

Fischer, David Hackett. *Albion's Seed: Four British Folkways in America.* New York: Oxford University Press, 1989.

Francke, Linda Bird. *Ground Zero: The Gender Wars in the Military.* New York: Simon and Schuster, 1997.

Frank, Jerome D., and Julia B. Frank. *Persuasion and Healing: A Comparative Study of Psychotherapy.* 1961. Baltimore: Johns Hopkins University Press, 1991.

Fromm, Erich. *The Art of Loving.* New York: Harper and Brothers, 1956.

Fuller, Margaret. *The Woman and the Myth: Margaret Fuller's Life and Writings.* 2nd ed. Ed. Bell Gale Chevigny. Boston: Northeastern University Press, 1994.

Geertz, Clifford. *The Interpretation of Cultures.* New York: Basic Books, 1973.

Gilligan, James. *Violence: Our Deadly Epidemic and Its Causes.* New York: Grosset-Putnam, 1996.

Gilmore, David D. *Manhood in the Making: Cultural Concepts of Masculinity.* New Haven: Yale University Press, 1990.

—— *Misogyny: The Male Malady.* Philadelphia: University of Pennsylvania Press, 2001.

Goldbart, Stephen, and David Wallin. *Mapping the Terrain of the Heart: Passion, Tenderness, and the Capacity to Love.* Reading, Mass.: Addison-Wesley, 1994.

Goldstein, Jeffrey H. *Why We Watch: The Attractions of Violent Entertainment.* New York: Oxford University Press, 1998.

Graham, Dee L. R., with Edna Rawlings and Roberta K. Rigsby. *Loving to Survive: Sexual Terror, Men's Violence and Women's Lives.* New York: New York University Press, 1994.

Greven, Philip. *The Protestant Temperament: Patterns of Child-Rearing, Religious Experience, and the Self in Early America.* New York: Knopf, 1977.

—— *Spare the Child: The Religious Roots of Punishment and the Psychological Impact of Physical Abuse.* New York, Vintage, 1992.

Griffin, Susan. *Pornography and Silence: Culture's Revenge against Nature.* New York: Harper and Row, 1981.

Griffith, Elizabeth. *In Her Own Right: The Life of Elizabeth Cady Stanton.* New York: Oxford University Press, 1984.

Grimké, Sarah. "Marriage." *Letters on the Equality of the Sexes and Other Essays.* Ed. Elizabeth Ann Bartlett. New Haven: Yale University Press, 1988.

Groth, A. Nicholas, and H. Jean Birnbaum. *Men Who Rape: The Psychology of the Offender.* New York: Plenum, 1979.

Gubar, Susan. "Representing Porn." *For Adult Users Only: The Dilemma of Violent Pornography.* Ed. Susan Gubar and Joan Hoff. Bloomington: Indiana University Press, 1989.

Hall, Jacquelyn Dowd. *Revolt against Chivalry: Jessie Daniel Ames and the Women's Campaign against Lynching.* New York: Columbia University Press, 1974.

Haller, John, and Robin Haller. *The Physician and Sexuality in Victorian America.* Urbana: University of Illinois Press, 1978.

Halttunen, Karen. *Murder Most Foul: The Killer and the American Gothic Imagination.* Cambridge, Mass.: Harvard University Press, 1998.

Harris, Trudier. *Exorcising Blackness.* Bloomington: Indiana University Press, 1984.

Hawthorne, Nathaniel. *The American Notebooks.* Ed. Claude M. Simpson. Columbus: Ohio State University Press, 1962.

—— *The Scarlet Letter.* Ed. William Charvat et al. Columbus: Ohio State University Press, 1962.

Hazelwood, Roy, Park Elliot Dietz, and Ann Wolbert Burgess. *Autoerotic Fatalities.* Lexington, Mass.: Heath, 1983.

Hazelwood, Roy, with Stephen G. Michaud. *Dark Dreams: Sexual Violence, Homicide and the Criminal Mind.* New York: St. Martin's, 2001.

Hedrick, Joan D. *Harriet Beecher Stowe: A Life.* New York: Oxford University Press, 1994.

Hemingway, Ernest. *A Farewell to Arms.* 1929. New York: Scribner, 1969.

Hendler, Glenn. "Pandering in the Public Sphere: Masculinity and the Market in Horatio Alger." *American Quarterly,* 48 (1996): 415–438.

—— "Tom Sawyer's Masculinity." *Arizona Quarterly,* 49 (1993): 33–59.

Henry, Portrait of a Serial Killer. Dir. John McNaughton. Perf. Michael Rooker, Tom Towles, and Tracy Arnold. MPI Home Video, 1989.

Herbert, T. Walter. *Dearest Beloved: The Hawthornes and the Making of the Middle-Class Family.* Berkeley: University of California Press, 1993.

Hoganson, Kristin L. *Fighting for American Manhood: How Gender Politics Provoked the Spanish-American and Philippine-American Wars.* New Haven: Yale University Press, 1998.

Hohenadel, Kristin. "Film Goes All the Way (In the Name of Art)." *New York Times,* July 1, 2001, section 2: 1, 20.

hooks, bell. *Ain't I A Woman: black women and feminism.* Boston: South End Press, 1981.

—— *All about Love: New Visions*. New York: William Morrow, 2000.

Horney, Karen. *Feminine Psychology*. Ed. with an intro. by Harold Kelman. New York: Norton, 1973.

—— *The Neurotic Personality of Our Time*. 1937. New York: Norton, 1964.

Horrocks, Roger. *Masculinity in Crisis*. New York: St. Martin's, 1994.

Hrdy, Sarah Blaffer. *Mother Nature: A History of Mothers, Infants, and Natural Selection*. New York: Pantheon, 1999.

Hunt, Lynn, ed. *The Invention of Pornography: Obscenity and the Origins of Modernity, 1500–1800*. New York: Zone, 1993.

Irigaray, Luce. *Democracy Begins between Two*. Trans. Kirsteen Anderson. New York: Routledge, 2001.

Isenberg, Nancy. *Sex and Citizenship in Antebellum America*. Chapel Hill: University of North Carolina Press, 1998.

Jacobson, Neil, and John Gottman. *When Men Batter Women: New Insights into Ending Abusive Relationships*. New York: Simon and Schuster, 1998.

James, Henry. "Hawthorne." 1879. In *The Shock of Recognition*, ed. Edmund Wilson. New York: Modern Library, 1943.

Jung, Carl G. "Anima and Animus." *Two Essays in Analytical Psychology*. Trans. R. F. C. Hull. Cleveland: World, 1953.

—— *Mysterium Coniunctionis: An Inquiry into the Separation and Synthesis of Psychic Opposites in Alchemy*. Trans. R. F. C. Hull. Bollingen Series XX, vol. 14. Princeton: Princeton University Press, 1989.

Kasson, John F. *Houdini, Tarzan, and the Perfect Man: The White Male Body and the Challenge of Modernity.* New York: Hill and Wang, 2001.

Katz, Jonathan Ned. *The Invention of Heterosexuality.* New York: Plume/Penguin, 1995.

Kaufman, Michael, ed. *Cracking the Armour: Power, Pain and the Lives of Men.* Toronto: Viking, 1993.

Keegan, John. *The Face of Battle: A Study of Agincourt, Waterloo and The Somme.* New York: Penguin, 1978.

—— *A History of Warfare.* New York: Knopf, 1993.

Kendrick, Walter. *The Secret Museum: Pornography in Modern Culture.* Berkeley: University of California Press, 1996.

Kerber, Linda. *Women of the Republic: Intellect and Ideology in Revolutionary America.* Chapel Hill: University of North Carolina Press, 1980.

Kimmel, Michael. *Manhood in America: A Cultural History.* New York: Free Press, 1996.

—— "Masculinity as Homophobia: Fear, Shame and Silence in the Construction of Gender Identity." *Toward a New Psychology of Gender.* Ed. Mary M. Gergen and Sara N. Davis. New York: Routledge, 1997.

Kimmel, Michael S., and Thomas E. Mosmiller, eds. *Against the Tide: Pro-Feminist Men in the United States, 1776–1990.* Boston: Beacon, 1992.

Kindlon, Dan, and Michael Thompson. *Raising Cain: Protecting the Emotional Life of Boys.* New York: Ballantine, 1999.

Kipnis, Laura. *Bound and Gagged: Pornography and the Politics of Fantasy in America*. New York: Grove, 1996.

Kivel, Paul. *Men's Work: Facilitator's Guide: A Complete Counseling Plan for Breaking the Cycle of Male Violence*. Center City, Minn.: Hazeldon, 1993.

—— *Men's Work: How to Stop the Violence That Tears Our Lives Apart*. New York: Ballantine 1992.

Kleinman, Arthur. *Rethinking Psychiatry: From Cultural Category to Personal Experience*. New York: Free Press, 1988.

Korten, David C. *When Corporations Rule the World*. West Hartford, Conn.: Kumarian, 1996.

Kramer, Lawrence. *After the Lovedeath: Sexual Violence and the Making of Culture*. Berkeley: University of California Press, 1997.

Lawrence, D. H. *Studies in Classic American Literature*. 1923. New York: Doubleday, 1951.

Leaming, Barbara. *If This Was Happiness: A Biography of Rita Hayworth*. New York: Viking, 1989.

Lears, Jackson. *No Place of Grace: Antimodernism and the Transformation of American Culture, 1880–1920*. New York: Pantheon, 1981.

Lefkowitz, Bernard. *Our Guys: The Glen Ridge Rape and the Secret Life of the Perfect Suburb*. New York: Vintage, 1997.

Lerner, Gerda. *The Female Experience: An American Documentary*. Indianapolis: Bobbs-Merrill, 1977.

Levant, Ronald F. "Nonrelational Sexuality in Men." *Men and Sex*. Ed. Levant and Brooks.

Levant, Ronald F., and Gary R. Brooks, eds. *Men and Sex: New Psychological Perspectives*. New York: Wiley, 1997.

Levant, Ronald F., with Gini Kopecky. *Masculinity Reconstructed: Changing the Rules of Manhood—at Work, in Relationships, and in Family Life*. New York: Dutton, 1996.

Levant, Ronald F., and William S. Pollack, eds. *A New Psychology of Men*. New York: Basic Books, 1995.

Leverenz, David. *Manhood and the American Renaissance*. Ithaca: Cornell University Press, 1989.

Lewis, R. W. B. *The American Adam: Innocence, Tragedy, and Tradition in the Nineteenth Century*. Chicago: University of Chicago Press, 1955.

Lindeman, Gerald F. *Embattled Courage: The Experience of Combat in the American Civil War*. New York: Free Press, 1987.

Lippard, George. *The Quaker City; or, The Monks of Monk Hall: A Romance of Philadelphia Life, Mystery, and Crime*. 1970. Amherst: University of Massachusetts Press, 1995.

Lisak, David. "Male Gender Socialization and the Perpetration of Sexual Abuse." *Men and Sex*. Ed. Levant and Brooks.

Macdonald, Andrew [William L. Pearce]. "Excerpts from One Right-wing Author's Script for the Future." *New York Times*, July 5, 1995: A18.

MacKinnon, Catherine A. *Only Words*. Cambridge, Mass.: Harvard University Press, 1993.

—— "Sexuality, Pornography and Method: 'Pleasure under Patriarchy.'" *Feminism and Political Theory*. Ed. Cass R. Sunstein. Chicago: University of Chicago Press, 1989.

Mailer, Norman. *An American Dream*. New York: Henry Holt, 1965.

—— *The Naked and the Dead*. New York: Henry Holt, 1948.

—— "The White Negro." *Advertisements for Myself*. Cambridge, Mass.: Harvard University Press, 1992.

Martin, Dell. *Battered Wives*. 1976. New York: Pocket Books, 1983.

Marx, Leo. *The Machine in the Garden: Technology and the Pastoral Ideal in America*. New York: Oxford University Press, 1964.

McNiell, William H. *The Human Condition: An Ecological and Historical View*. Princeton: Princeton University Press, 1980.

Melville, Herman. *White Jacket; or, The World in a Man-of-War*. Ed. Harrison Hayford, Hershel Parker, and G. Thomas Tanselle. Evanston: Northwestern University Press, 1970.

Messner, Michael. *Power at Play: Sports and the Problem of Masculinity*. Boston: Beacon, 1992.

Messner, Michael A., and Donald F. Sabo. *Sex, Violence and Power in Sports: Rethinking Masculinity*. Freedom, Calif.: Crossing Press, 1994.

Michaud, Stephen G. *Lethal Shadow: The Chilling True-Crime Story of a Sadistic Sex Slayer*. New York: Onyx Penguin, 1994.

Michaud, Stephen G., and Roy Hazelwood. *The Evil That Men Do: FBI Profiler Roy Hazelwood's Journey into the Minds of Sexual Predators*. New York: St. Martin's, 1998.

Millett, Kate. *Sexual Politics*. New York: Doubleday, 1970.

Moon, Michael. *Disseminating Whitman: Revision and Corporeality In* Leaves of Grass. Cambridge, Mass.: Harvard University Press, 1991.

Nack, William, and Lester Munson. "The Wrecking Yard." *Sports Illustrated*, 7 May 2001: 62–75.

Napier, Augustus Y. *The Fragile Bond: In Search of an Equal, Intimate and Enduring Marriage*. New York: HarperPerennial, 1990.

Nelson, Dana. *National Manhood: Capitalist Citizenship and the Imagined Fraternity of White Men*. Durham: Duke University Press, 1998.

Newfield, Christopher. "Democracy and Male Homoeroticism." *Yale Journal of Criticism*, 6 (1993): 30–62.

——— "The Politics of Male Suffering: Masochism and Hegemony in the American Renaissance." *differences: A Journal of Feminist Cultural Studies*, 1 (1989): 55–87.

Newman, Louise Michele. *White Women's Rights: The Racial Origins of Feminism in the United States*. New York: Oxford University Press, 1999.

Nissenbaum, Stephen. *Sex, Diet and Debility in Jacksonian America: Sylvester Graham and Health Reform*. Westport, Conn.: Greenwood, 1980.

Norris, Frank. *McTeague*. Ed. Donald Pizer. New York: Norton, 1977.

——— *Moran of the Lady Letty: A Story of Adventure off the California Coast*. New York: Doubleday, 1928.

—— *The Octopus.* Ed. Kenneth S. Lynn. Boston: Houghton Mifflin, 1958.

O'Brien, Tim. *If I Die in a Combat Zone, Box Me Up and Ship Me Home.* New York: Laurel, 1973.

—— *The Things They Carried.* New York: Penguin, 1990.

Ortner, Sherry B. "Gender Hegemonies." *Making Gender: The Politics and Erotics of Culture.* Boston: Beacon, 1996.

Osherson, Samuel. *Wrestling with Love: How Men Struggle with Intimacy.* New York: Fawcett, 1992.

Palac, Lisa. *The Edge of the Bed: How Dirty Pictures Changed My Life.* Boston: Little, Brown, 1998.

Peeping Tom. Dir. Michael Powell. Perf. Carl Boehm, Moira Shearer, Anna Massey, and Maxine Audley. Admit One Video Presentations, 1960.

Pleck, Joseph. "The Gender Role Strain Paradigm: An Update." *New Psychology of Men.* Ed. Levant and Pollack.

—— "Men's Power with Women, Other Men, and Society: A Men's Movement Analysis." *Against the Tide.* Ed. Kimmel and Mosmiller.

—— *The Myth of Masculinity.* Cambridge, Mass.: MIT Press, 1981.

Pollack, Vivian R. *The Erotic Whitman.* Berkeley: University of California Press, 2000.

—— "'In Loftiest Spheres': Whitman's Visionary Feminism." *Breaking Bounds: Whitman and American Cultural Studies.* Ed. Betsy

Erkkila and Jay Grossman. New York: Oxford University Press, 1996.

Pollack, William S. "No Man Is an Island: Toward a New Psychoanalytic Psychology of Men." *New Psychology of Men*. Ed. Levant and Pollack.

—— *Real Boys: Rescuing Our Sons from the Myths of Boyhood.* New York: Random House, 1998.

Pollack, William S., and Ronald F. Levant, "Coda: A New Psychology of Men: Where Have We Been? Where Are We Going?" *New Psychology of Men*. Ed. Levant and Pollack.

Psycho. Dir. Alfred Hitchcock. Perf. Anthony Perkins, Janet Leigh, Vera Miles, and John Gavin. Universal, 1960.

Real, Terrence. *I Don't Want to Talk about It: Overcoming the Secret Legacy of Male Depression.* New York: Scribner, 1997.

"The Regulation of Pornography: An Historical Perspective." *Final Report of the Attorney General's Commission on Pornography.* Nashville: Rutledge Hill Press, 1986, 303–310.

Reynolds, David. *Beneath the American Renaissance: The Subversive Imagination in the Age of Emerson and Melville.* New York: Knopf, 1988.

Rhode, Deborah. *Speaking of Sex: The Denial of Gender Inequality.* Cambridge, Mass.: Harvard University Press, 1997.

Rich, Adrienne. "When We Dead Awaken." *Adrienne Rich's Poetry and Prose.* Comp. and ed. Barbara Charlesworth Gelpi and Albert Gelpi. New York: Norton, 1993.

Rich, Frank. "Naked Capitalists." *New York Times Magazine*, 20 May 2001: 51–56, 80–82, 92.

Rosenberg, Charles, and Carroll Smith-Rosenberg, eds. *The Secret Vice Exposed! Some Arguments against Masturbation.* New York: Arno, 1974.

Rotundo, Anthony. *American Manhood: Transformations in Masculinity from the Revolution to the Modern Era.* New York: Basic Books, 1993.

Rousseau, Jean Jacques. *Emile, or On Education.* Intro., trans. Alan Bloom. New York: Basic Books, 1979.

Royster, Charles. *The Destructive War: William Tecumseh, Stonewall Jackson, and the Americans.* New York: Vintage, 1991.

—— *A Revolutionary People at War: The Continental Army and American Character, 1775–1783.* New York: Norton, 1979.

Ryan, Mary. *Cradle of the Middle Class: The Family in Oneida County, New York, 1790–1865.* Cambridge: Cambridge University Press, 1981.

Salter, Anna C. *Treating Child Sex Offenders and Victims: A Practical Guide.* Newbury Park, Calif.: Sage, 1988.

Sanday, Peggy Reeves. *Fraternity Gang Rape: Sex, Brotherhood, and Privilege on Campus.* New York: New York University Press, 1990.

—— *A Woman Scorned: Acquaintance Rape on Trial.* New York: Doubleday, 1996.

Schulhofer, Stephen. *Unwanted Sex: The Culture of Intimidation and the Failure of Law.* Cambridge, Mass.: Harvard University Press, 1998.

Schwartz, Pepper. *Love between Equals: How Peer Marriage Really Works*. New York: Free Press, 1994.

Scully, Diana. *Understanding Sexual Violence: A Study of Convicted Rapists*. London: HarperCollins, 1990.

"Seduction." *Christian Examiner*, 15 (Nov. 1833): 158–171.

Sellers, Charles. *The Market Revolution: Jacksonian America, 1815–1846*. New York: Oxford University Press, 1991.

Seltzer, Mark. *Serial Killers: Death and Life in America's Wound Culture*. New York: Routledge, 1998.

Shakespeare, William. *The Norton Shakespeare Based on the Oxford Edition*. Ed. Stephen Greenblatt et al. New York: Norton, 1997.

Silverberg, Robert Allan. *Psychotherapy for Men: Transcending the Masculine Mystique*. Springfield, Ill.: Charles Thomas, 1986.

Silverstein, Olga, and Beth Rashbaum. *The Courage to Raise Good Men*. New York: Penguin, 1994.

Sklar, Kathryn Kish. *Catharine Beecher: A Study in American Domesticity*. New Haven: Yale University Press, 1973.

Slotkin, Richard. *Regeneration through Violence: The Mythology of the American Frontier, 1600–1860*. Middletown, Conn.: Wesleyan University Press, 1973.

Smith, Henry Nash. *Virgin Land: The American West as Symbol and Myth*. Cambridge, Mass.: Harvard University Press, 1950.

"Southern Baptist Convention's Statement on the Family." *Baptist Faith & Message Article XVIII. The Family.* 11 May 2000 <www.youareright.org/sbc_statement.htm.>

Spillane, Mickey. *One Lonely Night.* 1951. New York: Signet, 1979.

Stoller, Robert, and I. S. Levine. *Coming Attractions: The Making of an X-Rated Video.* New Haven: Yale University Press, 1993.

Stoltenberg, John. *The End of Manhood: A Book for Men of Conscience.* New York: Plume, 1994.

—— *Refusing to Be a Man: Essays on Sex and Justice.* Portland, Ore.: Breitenbush, 1989.

Stowe, Harriet Beecher. *Life and Letters of Harriet Beecher Stowe.* Ed. Annie Fields. Boston: Houghton Mifflin, 1897.

—— *Uncle Tom's Cabin; or, Life among the Lowly.* 1852. Ed. Ann Douglas. New York: Penguin, 1981.

Thompson, William. *Appeal of One Half the Human Race, Women, against the Pretensions of the Other Half, Men.* London: Source Book Press, 1825.

Thoreau, Henry David. *Walden.* Riverside ed. Ed. Sherman Paul. Boston: Houghton Mifflin, 1960.

Tocqueville, Alexis de. *Democracy in America.* Vol. 2. New York: Knopf, 1976.

Traister, Bryce. "Academic Viagra: The Rise of American Masculinity Studies." *American Quarterly,* 52, no. 2 (June 2000): 274–304.

True Lies. Dir. James Cameron. Perf. Arnold Schwarzenegger and Jamie Lee Curtis. Lightstorm, 1994.

Walker, Lenore. *The Battered Woman*. New York: HarperPerennial, 1979.

Warner, Michael. "Homo-Narcissism; or, Heterosexuality." *Engendering Men: The Question of Male Feminist Criticism*. Ed. Joseph A. Boone and Michael Cadden. New York: Routledge, 1990, 190–206.

—— *The Trouble with Normal: Sex, Politics, and the Ethics of Queer Life*. Cambridge, Mass.: Harvard University Press, 2000.

West, Robin. "Pornography as a Legal Text." *For Adult Users Only: The Dilemma of Violent Pornography*. Ed. Susan Gubar and Joan Hoff. Bloomington: Indiana University Press, 1989.

Whitman, Walt. "A Woman Waits for Me." *Against the Tide*. Ed. Kimmel and Mosmiller, 299–300.

Wiebe, Robert H. *Self-Rule: A Cultural History of American Democracy*. Chicago: University of Chicago Press, 1995.

Wills, Garry. *John Wayne's America*. New York: Simon and Schuster, 1997.

—— *Lincoln at Gettysburg: The Words That Remade America*. New York: Simon and Schuster, 1992.

Winerip, Michael. "The Beauty of Beast Barracks." *New York Times Magazine*, 12 Oct. 1997: 46–53, 62–64, 95.

Wood, Gordon. *The Radicalism of the American Revolution*. New York: Knopf, 1992.

Wrangham, Richard, and Dale Peterson. *Demonic Males: Apes and the Origins of Human Violence*. Boston: Houghton Mifflin, 1996.

Wright, Richard. *Native Son and How "Bigger" Was Born.* Intro. Arnold Rampersad. New York: HarperPerennial, 1993.

—— *Savage Holiday.* Chatham, N.J.: Chatham Bookseller, 1954.

—— *Uncle Tom's Children.* 1936. New York: HarperPerennial, 1993.

Acknowledgments

It is a pleasure to acknowledge the assistance I've received from many sources in working on this project.

Carol Clover offered encouragement and guidance at the outset, and I've been supported throughout by the intellectual companionship of Evan Carton, Ann Congelton, Francis Hutchins, Dana Nelson, David Leverenz, and Warwick Wadlington.

I have received generous assistance from persons working on these issues in professional endeavors outside the academy: Sheriff Ed Richards, an expert in the interpretation of sexual crime scenes; Dr. Fred Dooley and Deanna Garza-Lewis, psychologists who specialize in providing therapy for wife-beaters and sex-offenders; the FBI's Roy Hazelwood and the crime writer Stephen Michaud; Pam Wilhoite and the staff of the Texas Council on Family Violence.

My colleagues at Southwestern have been a major resource, not least because our small-college setting is congenial to interdisciplinary research and teaching, and also because of the strength of our Women's Studies Program. Helene Meyers helped me get the project started, and the developing manuscript received comment from the Writers' Group, convened by Gwen Kennedy Neville and including Suzanne Chamier, Jan Dawson, Peter Gottschalk, Dan Hilliard, Melissa Johnson, Emily Northrop, Ken Roberts, Farley Snell, and Doug Wixson. Ed Kain and Maria Lowe, both sociologists with a specialization in the study of gender and the family, read the final manuscript in its entirety; Shannon Winnubst, a specialist in feminist theory, and Dr. Lee Edwards, Southwestern's staff psychologist, likewise provided helpful comments.

Serving on a campus Task Force on Sexual Harassment in 1988 was a major spur to this project, and my continued involvement in these issues on campus has yielded valuable insight. In this connection I want to thank Sherra Babcock, Deborah Brown, Gary Richter, Jeannie Watson, and Amanda Whitt.

The issues of this book have been the subject of vigorous classroom discussion (and dispute) in literature courses at Southwestern, where I have learned from students in ways that materially benefit the result. I'm indebted in particular to Terah Bowling, Enrique Garcia, Jonathan Grant, Rebecca Jamerson, Rachel Kunath, Cezanne McLoughlin, Yen Nguyen, Shireen Roshanravan, Jill Seeber, and Bret Starr.

I am also grateful to Southwestern University for research support throughout the project, and to the staff of the Smith Library Center at Southwestern, especially Lisa Anderson, Carol Fonken, Dana Hendrix, Joan Parks, and the student assistant Jennifer Fite.

A residency at the Rockefeller Foundation's Study Center at Bellagio, Italy, provided an ideal environment for interdisciplinary discussion. I learned a lot from conversations, sometimes contentious, with Gerald Weissman, Michael Roemer, Leon Litwack, Barbara Bergmann, and Ann Mayer.

Tim Beneke and Paul Kivel are pioneers. Their studies of the temperament that disposes men to commit sexual violence have been joined to activist programs that deserve endorsement and adoption nationwide. Both offered responses to my work and discussed with me a broad range of related issues.

Giles Gunn and Lindsay Waters aided in bringing the project to fruition.

For my wife, Marjorie Millard Herbert, my gratitude can only be intimated. Thirty-eight years of exploration and discovery at the bed-and-board frontier, where we've sought an equal and loving marriage, have yielded intellectual and spiritual wealth that there is no earthly way to sum up. The book is dedicated to my daughter, now a woman grown, who began to reshape my thinking about gender the moment she was born.

Index